AF522361

Revolution in Teaching Approach

Revolution in Teaching Approach

Edited by

Dr.A.MARIYAMMAL

Assistant professor

Sakthi institute of Teacher Education
and research Dindigul, Tamil Nadu

RANDOM PUBLICATIONS

NEW DELHI (INDIA)

Revolution in Teaching Approach

ISBN 978-93-5111-748-3

Published in 2015 in India by
RANDOM PUBLICATIONS
Reprint 2021
4376-A/4B, Gali Murari Lal, Ansari Road
New Delhi-110 002
Phone : +9111-43580356, 011-43142548, 011-23289044
e-mail : sales@randompublications.com
info@randompublications.com
randomexports@gmail.com

Type Setting by : Shah Computer Graphics, Delhi-110094
Printed at: Replika Press Pvt. Ltd.

Contents

3

4

5

6

7

8

12

13

14

15

16

28

29

30

1

Revitalization of Science Teacher Education

Introduction

The present educational scenario of the 21st century has become prone to stress more on Quality than on Quantity. The primary aim of every educational institution is to provide a good and quality education to the students. Unless we built a strong base we cannot think over and strength of the premise. Similarly the country which shows keen interest in providing the quality based education will surely empower the knowledge of the students and in turn it will lead to the development of the Nation. Moreover this century is known for the drastic development of Science and Technology. Day by day numbers of innovations are keeping on growing. It is the duty of the teacher to incorporate recent developments to the students that occur across the world. With an increased availability of the knowledge centers and a rapid rise in the enrolment of the students the responsibilities of the teachers also have increased many folds. In case of science teacher, the responsibility becomes more than the others. Meanwhile if the teacher has enough capability to maintain the larger group of students, then he/she becomes the successful teacher. For this, it is mandatory for the Science teacher to equip, empower, and update the knowledge every day. In this connection the author of this paper has planned to discuss the present status of the Science teacher education and tries to give some suggestions that can improve the quality of the science education in India.

A few decades back the science was given a step-motherly treatment and was considered to be a subject meant for less important subject. Science has now established its claim to be placed in a school curriculum. Due to its utilitarian, intellectual, vocational, cultural moral and aesthetic values it has been placed in the curriculum with due prestige. The training, the student receives in science during his study days can be applied to solve other problems in future life. Moreover the results of the science are generalizable and it does not give any room for superstitions and other facts without proofs. Teacher education is the vital for the development of the country and this is the age of science and technology. Proper science education is must for the advancement of the nation. Several committees have forwarded their suggestions for the development of the teacher education in general and science education in particular, but the standard of science education in India is still to come up to international standard. Unfortunately the present day of teaching science is far from being satisfactory. The education of science teachers is the main concern to be geared up, organized, revitalized and improved in order to shape the science education in the light of the present changing scenario of the educational world.

Problems in Selection of the Candidates

In present condition, the selection of the candidates for B.Ed program are being done on the basis of their academic marks scored in the graduation level. It is not actually valid and reliable. In order to select the qualified candidates, the exclusive selection procedures have to be done through entrance examination. For example, the theory examination may be conducted for 50 marks and the other 50 marks can be allotted for the interview. The theory exam can comprise of general mental ability test, aptitude test, attitude test and general awareness. The interview can be of checking the personality of the candidate, interest of the candidate towards science subject and etc., this kind of selection will ensure the quality of science education and prevent the unwanted entry of the incapable or uninterested candidate into the program.

Poor Knowledge in Preparing Lesson Plans

Due to the short period of the B.Ed program, the student teachers gain inadequate knowledge in preparing the lesson plans. This will lead to the poor performance of the candidate during teaching practice. As a good science teacher, it is must to know the procedure of writing the lesson plan in effective manner. To overcome this problem, the special classes can be handled by the subject experts to provide adequate knowledge in preparing good lesson plans. Copying from the previous year's record books has to be avoided. The concerned faculty member has to look into this concern strictly to avoid such malpractices.

Lack of Knowledge in Preparing and Handling Teaching Aids

As we know that audio-visual aids promote the teaching learning process so that every science teacher must possess good capability in preparing and handling the teaching aids wherever necessary. Unfortunately, considerable number of student teachers are interested in buying the readymade teaching aids available in markets or prepared by the third person. This will lead to the financial burden as well as poor knowledge in preparing teaching aids. The subject teacher should not entertain this practices and he can ask the student teachers to prepare such teaching aids by their own. Teaching aids can be effectively prepared with the help of available low cost materials. Moreover the student teachers have to be trained to utilize the teaching aids in effective manner.

Problems in Supervision during Practice Teaching

Every student teacher undergoes for practice teaching for at least 45 days in B.Ed Program. During practice teaching, the subject teacher must supervise the candidate's way of motivating the students, way of delivering the concepts, way of giving necessary examples, way of using teaching aids and etc.; Mistakes done by the student teacher can be corrected with the necessary instructions given by the subject teacher. But unfortunately, during practice teaching, the subject teachers could not find enough time to supervise each and every student teacher's teaching. In some institutions, during the practice teaching the subject teachers are assigned some official works or they take leave. This kind of thing should not be entertained. The authorities of institution should make strict measures in this concern.

Suggestions to Improve Science Teacher Education

1. The present one year B.Ed., program should be made of two years
2. Internship should be of six months instead of 45 days in practice teaching.
3. Scientific activities such as science fair, science club, museum, and exhibition can be encouraged.
4. College of education should be equipped with scientific materials and scientific instruments.
5. Seminars, conferences sand workshops related to science education can be organized every year by the institutions / colleges.
6. Job security should be provided to the selected and passed candidates by the government
7. Revision of curriculum should be made at a regular interval of time.
8. Suggestions from school science teacher and science teacher educators should be received in order to improve the system.
9. The teachers have to undergo for orientation programs, refresher courses every year in order to balance their ability with the recent developments.
10. The science teaching can be done with the help of innovative technologies like CAI, Video Packages etc., during the practice teaching.

11. Monitoring and evaluation should be made an integral part of teacher training program to know the strength, weakness, opportunities and Outcomes of the program.

12. All the existing college of educations should be accredited by NAAC.

Conclusion

In order to maintain the quality, the environment of the teacher education institutions should be improved. The science teacher educators should be given freedom to work. If there is any lacuna found in the system of such privately managed college of educations, their affiliations should be cancelled. NCTE is doing lot of commendable developments to improve the quality over nationwide. The relationship between the institution and the workers should be transparent and everyone should work to the betterment of the quality of education. In order to compete with the global knowledge market, the quality of education in our nation needs more betterment. This is becoming crucial for survival. So there is an urgent need to reform and revitalize the present education system for ensuring and creation of the quality of intellectual infrastructure in India.

References

1. Das, R.C. (1992): "Science teaching in Schools". Sterling Publishers private limited, New Delhi.
2. Deka, K.K. and Sharma, J.K. (1992): "Teacher education in the third world countries: India as a case study", The Educational Review, Chennai, pp. 201-205.
3. Krishna, D.G. and Rao, K.V.(1992) : "Effective Science Teaching: A trainers Paradigm", Journal of School science, NCERT, pp. 18-20.
4. Nadeen, N.A. (1989): Profile of Effective Teacher, Fulbright publishing company, Srinagar.
5. Panda B.N. & A.D.Tewari (2009): "Teacher Education", APH Publishing House, New Delhi. pp. 397-404.

2

Designing Learning Environment of Tomorrow Innovation in Teaching Learning Process

Education is the most important invention of mankind. It is more important than his invention of tools, machines, spacecraft, medicine, weapons and even of language, because language too was the product of his education. Information Communication Technology is the most powerful engine to accelerate the growth of developing countries. It is evident to equip the young generation with the skills of ICT so that they will be fit to meet the challenges ahead of them. Today school children are well exposed to T.V. shows, computer programs, video games, e-mail based information exchange, internet browsing and many other forms of educative entertainment. Using the experiences of the children as the base, providing further learning experience is a challenging task. Computers are often a catalyst for student activity. Internet also known as cyberspace or information super highway plays a vital role in education. One of the most powerful and rewarding instructional material at the fingertips of the learner is the internet. Within seconds an entire civilization of the country thousands of miles away is at your desktop. Internet is also an ideal mechanism for encouraging students to assume responsibility for their own learning. As students find different learning resources on the internet, they become active participants in their quest for knowledge. Students are able to define their learning needs, find information, assess its value, build their own knowledge base, and communicate their discoveries.

Traditional classroom techniques will not do justice to the learners of this generation. They require technique that will stimulate them to explore, discover and learn by themselves as much as possible and the role of teacher is to be an effective facilitator. Teachers should have the freedom to innovate, to devise appropriate methods of communication and activities relevant to the needs and capabilities and the concerns of the community, says National Educational Policy. The quality of education we provide to our children depends in large measure upon the quality of teachers we inject into the educational system other things remaining equal. The quality of teachers in turn depends on the quality of preparation they receive in our teacher training institutions.

Modern Media and Education

We live in the age of computers. There are growing demands on almost everyone, including the learning and teaching community to become technologically literate. Computers are often a catalyst for student activity. Internet also known as cyberspace or information super highway plays a vital role in education. One of the most powerful and rewarding instructional material at the fingertips of the learner is the internet. Within seconds an entire civilization of the country thousands of miles away is at your desktop. Internet is also an ideal mechanism for encouraging students to assume responsibility for their own learning. As students find different learning resources on the internet, they become active participants in their quest for knowledge. Students are able to define their learning needs, find information, assess its value, build their own knowledge base, and communicate their discoveries.

The implementation of different branches of technology in the information and communication processing is called information communication technology. Their application in education includes web based learning, e-tutoring, computer assisted instruction, computer managed instruction, tele-conferencing, interactive video, multimedia learning, satellite instructional television programme, edusat, reach the unreached, virtual classroom, e-book, digital library and electronic community etc.

Web-based learning

Web-based learning environments may be designed for students of distance education as well as conventional classroom students.

Principles of web-based learning

1. The learning experiences designed for web-based teaching must focus specific learning objectives and outcomes.
2. The learner should be actively engaged and made to feel the real-life experiences through simulation.
3. Keeping in mind the various learning styles of students, a variety of media are made use of to develop appropriately learning environment to achieve the desired learning out comes.
4. Learning environment must include both knowledge based as well as problem based learning.
5. Learning experiences must reflect the needs and interests of the community.

E-Learning

E-Learning includes different forms of technology enhanced learning such as online learning. E-learning is used to define a specific mode to attend a course or programmes of study where the students rarely or never meet face to face nor access on campus educational facilities, because they study online.

Advantages of e-learning

1. Improved performance – It has been proved that higher education students in online learning performed better than those in face to face courses.

2. Increased access – Instructors of the highest caliber can share their knowledge across borders, allowing students to attend courses across physical, political, and economic boundaries.
3. Convenience and flexibility to learners.

In many contexts e-learning is self-paced and the learning sessions are available 24x7. Learners are not bound to a specific day or time to physically attend classes. They can also pause learning sessions at their convenience.

E-tutoring

E-tutoring can be defined as teaching, support, management and assessment of students on programmes of study that involves significant use of online technology. Thus at first glance e-tutoring is only different to tutoring in terms of the involvement of technology. Herein, however, are contained vital differences in terms of time, distance and the specific technologies adopted, and these are all the Implications for teaching staff. The capabilities required can be quiet different to face to face teaching both in terms of integrating appropriate forms of technology into learning activities and in managing and supporting students' learning online .

Tele-Conferencing

In Tele-Conferencing, people situated at distant places establish direct contact through tele-communication and converse among themselves. In a tele-conferencing procedure all the three types of tele-conferencing such as audio, video and computer is integrated and supplements each other so that the participants get almost the feeling as if they are present physically in the conference.

Virtual-Education

Virtual education is a term describing online education using the internet. It refers to instruction in a learning environment where teacher and student are separated by time or space, or both, and the teacher provides course content through course management applications, multimedia resources, the internet, videoconferencing, etc. Students receive the content and communicate with the teacher via the same technologies.

Virtual course is similar to online course which is delivered on the internet. "Virtual" is used here to characterize the fact that the course is not taught in a classroom face to face but through some substitute mode that can be associated with classroom teaching that means people do not have to go to the real class to learn.

A virtual programme is a study program in which all courses or at least a significant portion of the courses are virtual courses.

A virtual classroom is a learning environment created in the virtual space. The virtual classrooms improve access to advanced educational experiences by allowing students and instructors to participate in remote learning communities using personal computers; and to improve the quality and effectiveness of education by using the computer to support a collaborative learning process. The explosion of the knowledge age has changed the context of what is learnt and how it is learnt – the concept of virtual classrooms is a manifestation of this knowledge revolution.

Instruction Modes for Virtual Education

- Video-based courses are like face-to-face classroom courses, with a lecturer speaking and PowerPoint slides or online examples used for illustration. Video-streaming technologies are used. Students watch the video by means of freeware or plug-ins (e.g. windows media player, real player).
- Audio-based courses are similar but instead of moving pictures only the sound track of the lecturer is provided. Often the course pages are enhanced with a text transcription of the lecture.
- Animated courses: enriching text-oriented or audio-based course material by animations is generally a good way of making the content and its appearance more interesting.
- Web-supported textbook courses are based on specific textbooks. Students read and reflect on the chapters by themselves. Review questions, topics for discussion, exercises, case studies, etc. are given chapter wise on a website and discussed with the lecturer.
- Peer-to-peer courses are courses taught "on-demand" and without a prepared curriculum. A new field of online education has emerged in 2007 through new online education platforms.

Homework assignments are normally submitted electronically, e.g. as an attachment on e-mail or uploaded to the system in a view complete. When help is needed, lecturers, tutors, or fellow students, or a help desk are available, just like in a real university, the difference is that all communication goes via electronic media.

Conclusion

In modern days media play a vital role in education. Virtual schools now exist all around the world. Some of these virtual schools have been integrated into public schools, where students sit in computer laboratory and do their work online. In other situations students can be completely home schooled, or they can take any combination of public or private home schooling and online classes.

Enlightened, emancipated and empowered teachers lead communities and nations in their march towards better and higher quality of life. They reveal and elaborate the secrets of attaining higher values in life and nurture empathy for the fellow beings. Teachers are the torch bearers in creating social cohesion, national integration and a learning society. They not only disseminate knowledge but also create and generate new knowledge. They are responsible for acculturating role of education. No nation can even marginally slacken its efforts in giving necessary professional inputs to its teachers and along with that due status to their stature and profession.

Remember: the Internet had its birth in the research and academic communities. It was created to allow the free and rapid flow of information to benefit higher learning. Let's recapture that focus in our work, and enrich our teaching in the process!

References

1. Andrews, R. (ed.) (2004), The Impact of ICT on Literacy Education. London, RoutledgeFalmer.
2. Cox, M. (1997), The Effects of Information Technology on Students' Motivation. Coventry, Council for Educational Technology.

3

Flipped classrooms learning

Introduction

The "flipped classroom" has been making waves in the educational world for some time now. The concept of the flipped classroom has become one of the hottest debates in the academic world among primary educators, professors, and administrators alike. As education-based technology and online platforms continue to grow and improve, more and more devices, programs, and concepts are entering the educational world and shaking things up. Where at one time the concept of online learning, computer-based assignments, and the virtual classroom were scoffed at, today online education and technology in the classroom are top priorities for schools, teachers, and researchers.

Within our increasingly digital world, most of us agree that education must respond to the changing atmosphere of society. We accept that online learning and certain academic technologies are worthwhile. However, with education and learning, this flipped classroom remains both positives and negatives to the approach.

One of the hottest trends in education today is the flipped classroom: Computer-savvy students turn to online videos for the content normally taught in class and use class time to collaborate in discussion with peers and instructors. A flipped classroom is fundamentally about upending of time on task. Instead of holding forth each day at the front of a classroom the traditional notion of the "sage on a stage" teachers convert their lectures to videos, slide shows or audio lessons that can be watched or heard by students at home or elsewhere via the Internet or other information transfer tools, such as DVDs and thumb drives.

Flipped classroom education

The reason flipped classrooms are improving education around the world is because the role of the teacher has been flipped from a lecturer to a tutor. The focus of the classroom transforms one-size fits all instruction into individualized coaching.

What Does a Flipped Classroom Look Like?

Flipped Classroom will certainly look very different from a traditional classroom. Instead of students sitting in individual desks facing the front while their teacher lectures, students sit at tables or desks pushed together or are off by themselves doing work. Students are out of their seats, accessing books, computers and others students for information. Although a Flipped Classroom may appear chaotic, loud, or even messy at first glance, the action and collaboration taking place in this non-traditional classroom is a direct result of student learning. Have fun physically setting up your classroom for a flip by providing areas for group and individual learning and don't forget to involve students in the new Flipped Classroom design.

Flipped Classroom Model

The flipped classroom model is revolutionizing teaching methods and strategies around the globe, addressing these concerns by creating time for individualized 1:1 instruction between teachers and students.

Flipped classrooms are a reversed teaching model that "flips" the settings for instruction and homework. In a flipped class, instruction is provided to students at home through video or Internet based lectures and class time is used to complete homework-like assignments. By moving instruction to the home and homework to the class, students are given more 1:1 time with their teacher to work through their assignments. This 1:1 time helps to ensure that each student fully understands the key concepts presented in each lesson plan before moving on to the next lesson.

Here's how it works

1. Teachers provide students with digital instruction to watch at home (or after school)
2. Students watch the instruction to familiarize themselves with concepts to be covered in class the following day
3. Students spend class time completing assignments, based on the previous night's instruction, with the assistance of teachers
4. Students with a firm grasp of the lesson are encouraged to move on, and students who need assistance have a teacher readily available to help

Benefits of flipped classroom

1. More efficient for teachers: While there is an initial up-front investment that teachers have to make to set up a flipped classroom – creating a video can take 15 minutes or two days – they can ultimately save a lot of time using this model. In the future, recorded lesson plans and collected resources can be easily transferred to other classes. Plus, if students miss a class, teachers don't have to spend time going over missed material because it's all online.
2. Students control their learning: Research has shown that we all learn in different ways and at different speeds. If students are learning content at home, they can take their time to read through a passage, re-watch a video lecture or even initiate a Google search to better understand an idea. Instructors can also post multiple kinds of materials so that students are more likely to find a source that will help them, whether it's an article, video or interactive tool.

3. Inexpensive for schools to implement: Besides investing in a new video cameras or better classroom computers, the only other thing you need is time. This model is much more cost-effective for schools than purchasing hundreds of new classroom gadgets to increase engagement.
4. Versatile, engaging way to share content: One of the greatest things about this model is that teachers can share so many different kinds of content. Learning isn't restricted to a whiteboard or textbook. Instead, students can be directed to any website, mobile application or other kind of content. Teachers can create learning modules that allow students to quickly jump from one resource to the next.
5. Students—including special education students—having difficulty with concepts can pause and rewind the videos to give themselves extra time to parse out what a teacher means. "That's one of the most powerful things about these videos: that students who process slower, can process slower,"

Administrator role in implementing flipped learning

"Absolutely, they are critical as instructional leaders and lead learners in their schools," "They can support innovation, provide collaborative time and professional development, assign resources to innovative teachers, communicate with parents about new teaching strategies, and provide feedback and a view from outside the classroom.

The primary reason administrators balk at flipped learning is a lack of familiarity: "They need more information about how it works the issues that come up like how to evaluate flipped-learning teachers, the problems of rolling it out."

Administrators says that flipped learning can greatly increase a teacher's ability to provide differentiated instruction given that students work at their own pace in the classroom—and teachers can provide more challenging work for those who are breezing through.

Administrators also continue to support the use of video within instruction and believe that it has an important role within classrooms today and tomorrow. Approximately one quarter of school principals indicated that their teachers are using videos they found online or creating their own Videos as part of their flipped learning model implementation. And thinking ahead to the next generation of classroom teachers, some of the principals said that they want pre service teachers to learn how to create and use videos and other digital media within their teacher preparation programs.

Advantage of flipped classroom learning

Students are able to approach material and take it in at their own speed. By covering lecture material at home and from a video-based platform, students can privately view the material. This allows them to approach things at their own pace without worry of peers noticing them moving slower or faster. Students can stop, pause, rewind, and fast forward material so that they can examine things in their own way.

By taking the lecture portion of the classroom home with them, students are able to utilize their teachers' one-on-one attention more successfully in the classroom. Students sit through lecture, gather questions, and prepare themselves for the day with the teacher to tackle "homework". Because the actual exercises are done in the classroom rather than at home with this model, students have their teacher available for questions with problems when they occur.

The flipped classroom also allows teaching to adapt more easily to the different teaching styles that individual students may be most successful with. By putting lectures in a video format, students can listen to the lesson and watch the video illustrate the lesson. Of course, this largely depends on how successful the actual video lecture is. You want a lecture (like the Khan videos) that explains concepts verbally, but also draws them out in images and pictures. This provides adequate learning opportunities for verbal learners and for visual learners. With in-classroom lecturing, the visual aspect of lecturing can be significantly more difficult to accomplish.

Disadvantage of flipped classroom learning

Classroom lecturing works better for some and doesn't work for others; the flipped classroom method is not going to accommodate every individual perfectly. The biggest setback today to the flipped classroom method is that not all students and schools have access to technologies that can really work for this method.

Students from lower income areas and lower income families may not have access to the computers and internet technologies that the flipped classroom requires. The structure really hinges on every student having personal access to his or her own personal device. This simply is not the case for every student and every school district. Students who do not have personal home computers or access to the internet would be forced to use public computers at a library or at the school. This, to some degree, eliminates the personal and private experience of taking in the lecture. What makes having lectures as homework so powerful is that students can do it on their own time and in their own way. At a library computer or school computer time limits typically exist and access can be limited if it is busy. This is problematic.

Another downside to the idea of the flipped classroom that many people bring up is the fact that students would be spending all of their "homework time" plugged-in in front of a computer screen. Not only do not all students do well with learning from a screen, but this also adds to a student's time in front of a screen and sitting inactively. While this concern isn't singular to the flipped classroom, the teaching concept doesn't help our young students to get up and get away from their computers, televisions, and iPods.

Conclusion

Flipped classroom learning are shifting the way teachers provide Instruction by inverting traditional teaching methods to engage students in the learning process. Using technology, lectures are moved out of the classroom and delivered online as a means to free up class time for interaction and collaboration. In order to effectively implement a flipped classroom, teachers must possess a set of requisite technical skills, conceptual knowledge and pedagogical expertise.

References

1. Bergmann, J., J. Overmyer, and B. Wilie. 2011. "The Flipped

Class: Myths Vs. Reality." http://www.thedailyriff.com/articles/the-flipped-class-conversation-689.php.

2. Hertz, M. 2012. "The Flipped Classroom: Pro and Con." *Edutopia*. http://www.edutopia.org/blog/flipped-classroom-pro-and-con-mary-beth-hertz.
3. Makice, K. 2012. "Flipping the Classroom Requires More Than Video | GeekDad | Wired.com." *GeekDad*. http:// www. wired. com/geekdad/2012/04/flipping-the-classroom/.
4. Strayer. 2007. "The Effects of the Classroom Flip on the Learning Environment: a Comparison of Learning Activity in a Traditional Classroom and a Flip Classroom That Used an Intelligent Tutoring System". Thesis, Ohio State University. http://etd.ohiolink.edu/view.cgi/Strayer%20Jeremy.pdf?osu1189523914.
5. Strayer, J. 2011. "The Flipped Classroom: Turning the Traditional Classroom on Its Head." http://www.knewton.com/flipped-classroom/.

4

Learning Without Limits

Introduction

As early as 1916 when John Dewey published his seminal work "Democracy and Education", it was acknowledged that learners should become active participants in the educational process. From this proposition it clearly follows that in learning from their own experience, students become, in a sense, their own teachers. The changed role of the learner has, in turn, implications for that of the teacher. Instead of the source of knowledge, teachers become facilitators of the learning process; that is, their role is to create the set of conditions under which students can best learn from their experiences. Moreover, teachers can fulfill this role only by becoming learners themselves, and a primary source of their learning must be their students. Simply put, teachers who learn become better teachers, and learners who teach become better learners. Although this idea seems straightforward enough, educators have been very slow to put it into practice. However, the rapid technological changes of the last few decades may well provide the catalyst food that finally brings about these needed reforms in the field of education.

Good teachers design learning

Recently, when I perused my twitter feed, I came upon a blog post titled Teacher as Learning Designer. Andrew Miller, the author, states: "If you are a teacher and you are trying to explain what you do, say, 'I am a learning designer!' Teachers need to be empowered with a variety of instructional designs to meet the needs of all students. They need to be honored for their expertise to create creative and engaging learning environments. We can re-frame the concept of "teaching" to truly encapsulate all that teachers can and should do!"

The way teachers teach their students has, I believe, a direct correlation to the way in which they learn themselves. We have all read in the latest teaching journals that teachers of today have to be devoted to lifelong learning. But what does that mean, really? What elements affect teacher learning and then in turn affect how that teacher teaches?

Eight influences on teacher learning

Louise Stoll, Jan McKay, et. al, in an 1999 presentation about influences on teacher learning (summarized at the New Zealand Ministry of Education website) described eight features that impact how a teacher learns.

Life and career experience. Life experiences do affect the way we learn. I was personally challenged when I had to teach soil characteristics to inner city students. These students hadn't had experience of playing in dirt as I had as a child in the suburbs. My students' life experiences were very different than mine in so many ways. In order to engage them in the process of learning, I had to understand what their life was all about. I did that by listening to their stories and their experience.

Personal Beliefs. What a teacher believes about a learning concept or a new teaching style greatly influences whether or not that teacher implements the idea. How many teachers were tuned out to early implementation of technology because of the belief that "technology integration is a fad", or "the way I've taught this unit has been fine for the last 20 years"? Personal attitudes, I believe, do color the words an instructor uses and the manner by which he/she approaches the topic.

Emotional Well Being: A lot had been written on the importance of emotional intelligences with regards to student learning. But, what about an instructor and his or her well being? Show me a teacher who has enough self confidence to fail in front of the class, and I will show you a teacher who can help his/her students learn to succeed by building on failure. Show me a teacher who is not fearful of fiascos and I will show you an educator who is not hesitant to use new technology.

Knowledge: This is a multifaceted aspect to learning since it relates not only to the specific content of the curriculum but also to teaching strategies, different types of learner intelligences, and even interpersonal and intrapersonal skills. The teacher who is equipped with a wide understanding of these topics can create an environment that truly supports every learner in their quest to discover the truth.

Skills: This is the "tool belt" that is the arsenal for any good teacher. The tools include different modes of engaging students such as, but not limited to, project based learning, cooperative learning, and peer review. Educators should be skillful enough to alter any style of teaching to meet the specific learning needs of the students.

Motivation to learn: "Motivation is the starting point for learning. For a busy and often overworked teacher to devote effort to change and new learning, there has to be a good reason for the change: some sort of catalyst or urgency – a sense that 'what I'm doing doesn't seem to be working.'" We can all look over the history of our teaching practice and recall times when we were motivated to learn something new because the old way just didn't work.

Personal Confidence: Face it, sometimes teaching can be likes mud wrestling; it's messy and exhausting! But the educator who believes that the job of teaching is worth the effort shakes off the mud and makes a difference in the lives of those is taught.

Sense of Interdependence: I used to be the Queen Mother, Judge, Arbitrator and Center of my classroom. Then I began to shift ownership of learning to my students. With the added presence of technology, my classroom became a hub that had spoken in all parts of the world. Collaboration, creativity, team building, and collegial aptitudes are now huge elements in the culture of my students' learning experience.

In a nutshell, today's teacher needs to be able to learn continuously from their students as they present the curriculum. To quote Anna from Mister God, This is Anna, "in the dark you have to describe yourself. In the daylight other people describe you." Educators have to be comfortable about being in the dark and journeying to the light by learning with students.

To learn without limit

More recently, technology has drastically changed how students learn in and out of the classroom. Teachers can no longer pretend to have all of the answers because students have an immense amount of knowledge at their fingertips with the internet; more specifically, Web 2.0 enables students to be not only learners but also teachers. all users not only to post comments, articles, and reports on the internet but also to edit and respond to those articles and reports. Teachers can use wikis in their classrooms and have groups of students work together or individually to research and become experts on a topic and then post their reports on the internet for all to read and learn from. This new area of education is allowing all students to become the teachers to not only the students in their classes but to the world. Any student who is interested and wishes to explore and research a particular topic is able to do so and publish his or her work. This not only increases the motivation to do a good job, but since anyone can go in and edit the work, it helps students to be flexible and open to new ideas and procedures. This technology also enables any topic to be approached from multiple perspectives. Students in the past have grown up learning subjects such as history from only one biased perspective. Now, individuals will be able to help contribute to online textbooks and add sections about topics that have never before been taught in the public schools. This technology will revolutionize our education system as it becomes more widely used and accepted (Alexander, 2006; Standen, 2006).

Conclusion

Largely as a result of technological change, the forces of globalism, multiculturalism, and multimodal's have conspired to transform and ultimately enrich the roles of both teacher and learner. As teachers extend their learning, learners can claim full ownership of their knowledge in the process of teaching it to others. This results in more effective teachers as well as a greater depth of understanding in students. This model of mutual learning can reform the educational system from within and help it to realize maximum benefits for both teachers and learners.

5

Learning Environment of the Speech Disordered

Introduction

Speech disorder is a widespread disabling problem which is associated with very adverse, long term outcome affecting the individual's family, academic and vocational achievements. Many attempts have been made by doctors, speech language pathologist, researchers, educationists etc to identify the causes of speech disorders to intervene it and to assist all who are working with the speech disordered to understand their problem better in all aspects of their everyday living experiences. This article is intended to be guidelines for speech-language pathologists, audiologists, parents, teachers, administrators, school boards, architects, and building contractors. It contains minimum requirements for creating optimal learning environments for students and is designed to be a substantiating reference for use when building a new school, redesigning an already existing structure, and/or advocating for improvement of facility work conditions. The ultimate goal of this article is to be a reference guide for providing the best learning environment which will contribute to the overall success of students.

Adequate working conditions and facilities in schools for teachers, speech-language pathologists and audiologists have always been acknowledged as an essential one for creating an optimal learning environment for the children with speech impediments, but the quality of work settings and equipment varies widely in schools around the country. Implementation of the Individuals with Disabilities Education Act Amendments of 1997 (IDEA '97) increased school administrators' awareness of the importance of providing adequate learning environments for children with disabilities, including those with speech-language-hearing disorders.

Common Practices in School for Learning

Learning environment is commonly designed as listed below for the speech disordered:

1. Teachers will want to reduce un-necessary classroom noise as much as possible. This helps the child focus without contending with the extraneous noises which assists understanding and comprehension.
2. Be sure to be near the student when giving vocal instructions and ask the student to repeat the instructions and prompt when necessary. Provide verbal clues often.
3. Provide a quiet spot for the student to work whenever possible.
4. Speak slowly and deliberately.
5. Provide visual cues-on the blackboard or chart paper.
6. Focus the student frequently and provide step by step directions -repeating when necessary.
7. Use gestures that support understanding.
8. Avoid correcting speech difficulties - this will lead to a weaker self esteem, it's much more important to model correct speech patterns.
9. Touch base with the speech/language pathologist to ensure the correct accommodations are in place.
10. The learning environment needs to be positive.

11. Capitalize on the student's strengths as much as possible.
12. Be patient when the child is speaking, rushing a child with difficulties magnifies the frustration level.
13. Classrooms should include appropriate and comfortable visual, auditory, and physical access to information for learning. It is very vital to provide an acoustical environment for the speech disordered.

Besides the above mentioned best practices it is recommended to have a speech – language pathology room, equipment and furniture for providing a good learning environment for the speech disordered.

The space provided for speech-language pathology services in a regular school building should be located in the instructional area of the building that houses children of comparable age. It should be located in an area that ensures privacy, confidentiality, and sensitivity to student needs. The room should be used by only one professional at a time and should be designated for the exclusive use of the speech-language pathologist when he or she is scheduled to be in the building.

When services are provided outside the classroom setting, the area should be reasonably exclusive and large enough to provide the full range of evaluation and instructional activities needed to provide services to a caseload. These services may include evaluation and testing of individual students, pull-out treatment for individuals and/or groups, team meetings, and confidential conferences with teachers and parents, as well as activities to prepare for treatment, prepare and maintain assistive technology support, and provide case management services.

Each speech-language area should be readily accessible to no ambulatory students and should accommodate the special needs of students with disabilities. This includes students who are physically challenged, and students with low vision or neurological problems.

The facilities should be adequately heated and cooled, lighted and ventilated, and provided with sufficient electrical outlets and computer accessibility. Speech-language services should be provided in an environment that ensures student safety and welfare; complies with applicable building and safety codes; and includes universal precautions, infection control, risk management, and emergency preparedness

Each speech-language area should be large enough to accommodate the use and storage of special equipment and teaching materials. There should be an adequate number of age-appropriate desks/tables and chairs to meet the physical needs of students and parents, and for preschool, furniture and equipment to provide a developmentally appropriate curriculum.

The facility should be equipped with instructional aides (e.g., mirror, chalkboard/erase board, and bulletin board) that meet the needs of the students' individualized education programs (IEPs) and adequate office equipment and supplies, including a telephone. Speech-language pathologists should be provided with materials, technology devices, Internet access, and computer and technology support, as well as software for providing, managing, and monitoring services.

Each speech-language pathologist should have available current evaluation and instructional materials and equipment appropriate for the age, developmental ability, and disability condition of each student. These should include a variety of multimedia learning/curriculum materials, tests, and equipment, readily available for use to meet the individual interests and learning abilities of the students receiving services.

School districts should make available one portable individual audiometer for the speech-language pathologist to use for screening; this should be checked and calibrated annually in accordance with minimum audio logic standards. Best practice would include impedance screening by a speech-language pathologist trained by an audiologist. Also, one portable tape recorder and a supply of tapes; one portable auditory training unit, computer, and printer; one hearing aid battery tester; and assistive technology devices should be available. There should be adequate maintenance and prompt repair of all special equipment utilized for children with disabilities.

Interior Classroom

In a brief note how the interior structure of the classroom for the speech disordered is as follows:

Ceilings

A ceiling height of 9–12 feet is optimal for the listening environment. It is important to install acoustical ceiling tile that has a sound absorption coefficient rating that is sufficient to achieve the desired noise and/or reverberation reduction. Banners, student work, and plants suspended from the ceiling can contribute to the reduction of noise and reverberation

Floors

Although carpeting is an excellent means to reduce noise and reverberation, concerns do exist regarding indoor air quality and allergic reactions that carpeting may generate in a classroom setting. Carpeting, particularly if it is installed over a pad, is the most efficient and effective acoustical modification for absorbing excessive reverberation of high-frequency consonant sounds and dampening noise from students and movement of classroom furniture. The thickness of the pad contributes to the overall decrease in the amount of noise and reverberation.

Windows

Windows are highly reflective surfaces, and acoustical treatment may be provided by adding draperies, acoustically treated blinds, or shades. Double-pane windows offer more protection from outside noise than traditional windows, and closed windows allow far less noise to enter the classroom from adjacent or external noise sources.

Walls and Doors

Reflective wall surfaces may be treated in a variety of ways to dampen classroom noise and reverberation. Interior wall modifications, such as acoustical panels, cork, felt, or flannel bulletin boards, are useful in reducing noise and reverberation time. A well-fitted, solid-core door with a noise lock or doorway treatment will help to lessen noise from external or adjacent sources.

Seating and Furniture Arrangement

The human body absorbs sound. When desks and tables are staggered, sound will not travel directly to hard reflective surfaces such as walls, chalkboards, and windows. Felt or rubber caps or tennis balls can be used on chair and table legs to help reduce noise in classrooms, particularly if they are uncarpeted. Also, the classroom should be arranged so that instruction occurs away from noise sources (e.g., HVAC systems, aquariums) and to accommodate the teacher's instructional style. This will help reduce noise and the distance between the teacher and the students. Open plan rooms should be avoided whenever possible, particularly for students with hearing loss or other auditory deficits.

Heating, Ventilation, and Air Conditioning Systems

Supply and return ducts for heating and cooling systems may be treated with acoustical duct lining. If the classroom has an external HVAC system, as is the case with most portable classrooms, the main instructional areas should be planned away from this area if the HVAC system is a source of noise. Noise control devices (e.g., duct silencers, adequate duct length, vibration isolators) can be used in HVAC systems to achieve desirable noise levels in classrooms. When renovation or new construction is planned, careful consideration should be given to the selection and design of the school's HVAC system.

Lighting

Some fluorescent lighting systems emit a constant noise. Regular maintenance should be employed; ballasts can become noisy and create a 60 dB 1000 Hz (or thereabouts) hum. When lighting is housed above the acoustical tile ceiling, the noise level will be lessened.

Special Purpose Areas

Classrooms for students with hearing loss should be located away from high-noise sources. Mobile bulletin boards and bookcases may be placed at angles to the walls to decrease reverberation in the classroom. In areas where younger children are handling manipulative or playing with toys, covering the table surface with fabric will reduce noise levels. Study carrels can be lined with acoustic tiles, or rubber pads may be installed underneath equipment (e.g., computer, typewriter) to reduce noise in these areas.

In general Speech Disorders are very fatal and devastating where speech therapy works for regaining the speech but some conditions and diseases cannot be cured and the regaining of the speech may be lost permanently. Therefore early intervention is crucial and the best learning environment is in need for the development of the speech disordered.

References

1. Damico Jack, S., Muller Nicole, and Ball Martin, J., (2010). The Handbook of Language and Speech Disorders, United Kingdom: Blackwell Publishing Ltd, pp.50-51.
2. Umadevi,M.R.,(2010). Special Education: A Practical Approach to Educating Children With Special Needs, Hyderabad: Neelkamal Publications Pvt Ltd, pp.173-182.
3. Williams Dale. F, (2006). Stuttering Recovery: Personal and Empirical Perspectives, London: Lawrence Erlbaum Associates, pp.10.
4. Williams Lynn. A, (2003). Speech Disorders: Resource Guide for Pre School Children, New York: Singular Publishing Group, pp. 30-36.

6

Role of Ict in Educational Transactions

Introduction

The role of teachers is enormous, especially for nurturing children in their formative years, when they begin their schooling. Hence, it is very crucial to have qualified teachers to ensure prefect development of students. The various objectives of the ICT in Teacher Education, are to provide high quality education, monitor Teacher Education as approved by National Council for Teacher Education at all levels in the State, to develop research facilities in Teacher Education; The Tamil Nadu Teacher Education University from 2008, is very much focused to promote quality in Education and to standardize the system of operation. This paper focused on EDUSAT, INSAT, SITE, CAI, Video Conferencing, Virtual Classroom and the equipments and the UGC Tele programmes. Whatever it me, the today's student teachers are tomorrow's Teachers. So that, we are in need of utilization of media and technology in out classrooms and it can used in future for our educational transactions.

Teachers play a vital role in the overall growth and development of students. Teaching as profession is not only restricted to imparting academic knowledge, but also inculcating the right principles and values to the students. The role of teachers is enormous, especially for nurturing children in their formative years, when they begin their schooling. Hence, it is very crucial to have qualified teachers to ensure prefect development of students. Today, there are enormous colleges and universities in India that offer Courses in Education and Teacher Science.

As the needs of primary students are completely different from secondary students, the primary teachers and the secondary teachers are required to take different teachers 'training courses. Hence, most of the prominent Teacher training institutes offer different Courses which include Junior Basic Training or JBT, Basic Training Certificate or BTC, Primary Teachers Training or PTT, Bachelor of Education or B.Ed, Diploma in Education or D.Ed, and many other teachers training courses.

National Council of Teacher Education was established in 1973 by the Govt. of India. It was formed as advisory organization to government, on issues related to the teacher education. The government formed a National Policy on Education in 1986, which was aimed at setting up statutory body to provide quality Teachers' training in country, as step towards producing quality teaching professionals in India. In the year 1995, NCTE was awarded the status of statutory body in the pursuance of the National Council for Teacher Education Act. This Council sets the standards and norms for teachers' training right from primary teacher's education to post graduation teachers education. In the past, a teacher who wanted to display information for a classroom full of students had only a few options at his disposal: writing everything out on the chalkboard manually or projecting it onto a screen using a transparency projector. Today, the liquid crystal display (LCD) technology becoming common in homes has also made its way into the classroom.

Utilization of EDUSAT in Schools of Tamil Nadu

The NCERT acts as a major agency for implementing the bilateral Cultural Exchange Programmes with other countries in the field of school education also in addition to research, development, training, extension, and publication and dissemination activities. INSAT

(Indian National Satellites) are a series of satellites projected and maintained by ISRO for multipurpose space applications. INSAT-3B, INSAT-3C are satellites in this series.

The ISRO launched a Satellite for education, termed as EDUSAT. With the launch of EDUSAT, TV, Radio and data transfer has become easy for educational institutions situated all over the country. Quality education is to be provided to school students especially in rural areas through this Satellite. This will also enable high quality in-service training to school teachers in the state. Live programmes are being broadcast through the studio at Anna University using EDUSAT. For proper utilization of EDUSAT, a plan of action has been formulated. Satellite Interactive Terminals have been set up in all 29 District Institutes of Education and Training. Satellite interactive terminals will be established in all the BRCs, 215 Urban Cluster Resource Centers and 2000 Government High and Higher Secondary Schools in this academic year 2006-2007 in a phased manner under the aegis of SSA.

Some schools like Delhi Public School and IGNOU are already experimenting with teaching through lessons prepared for distance teaching using multimedia, slides etc. The communication technology based teaching is a viable solution. Any institution which can afford and is willing to put the efforts and costs involved, can utilize the technology. But the technology is still quite expensive and state has to support the venture. Of course the country may look forward to the institutions that have expertise in the related fields at the right time, for the better utilization.

SITE and its Uses

Satellite Instructional Television Experiment (SITE) (1975).This project, one of the largest techno-social experiments in human communication, was commissioned for the villagers and their Primary School going children of selected 2330 villages in six states of India. It started on August 1, 1975 for a period of one year in six states Rajasthan, Karnataka, Orissa, Bihar, Andhra Pradesh and Madhya Pradesh. The main objectives of this experiment were to study the process of existing rural communications, the role of television as new medium of education, and the process of change brought about by the community television in the rural structure with following two type of telecast: (i) Developmental education programmes in the area of agriculture and allied subjects, health, family planning and social education, which were telecast in the evening for community viewing and (ii) The school programmes of 22 ½ minutes duration each in Hindi, Kannada, Oriya and Telugu were telecast on each school day for rural primary school children of 5- 12 years age group to make the children realize the importance of science in their day to day life.

SITE experiment showed that the new technology made it possible to reach number of people in the remotest areas. The role of television was appreciated and it was accepted in rural primary schools as an educational force (IGNOU, 2000). Post-SITE project (1977).The target group for this post SITE project was the villagers of Rajasthan. This was a SITE continuity project and was initiated in March 1977 when a terrestrial transmitter was commissioned at Jaipur. The main objectives of SITE continuity project were to; (i) Familiarize the rural masses with the improved and scientific know how about farming, the use of fertilizers and the maintenance of health and hygiene; (ii) Bring about national and emotional integration; and (iii) Make rural children aware of the importance of education and healthy environment. This project was also successful.

Mass media serve some important functions. They are helpful in teaching large number of people. They are helpful in the spread of compulsory education and adult literacy. Recently their use is being made increasingly in distance education. They are useful in making instructions more effective and meaningful. Mass media play a pivotal role in education. It may be hardware approach like radio, tape recorder, television etc or soft ware approach like newspapers books , magazines etc. Mass media include Computer, Educational satellite, VCR and T.V to meet the tremendous challenges in the educational field using of multimedia is inevitable. In fact it is essential for the ever changing educational field.

The Barriers to Verbal Classroom Communication in the Classroom are;

(1) Inaudibility of speech

(2) Abnormal speed of speech

(3) Unfamiliar pronunciation of the teacher.

(4) Use of unfamiliar words and technical terms without explanations

(5) Lack of understanding of the basic knowledge of the students known as referent confusion

(6) Day dreams on the part of the students on account of their inattentiveness.

(7) Unsystematic presentation of the subject matter

(8) Lack of scope of immediate feedback

(9) Lack of physical facilities in the classroom

(10) Socio-economic and cultural difference among the students.

Video Conferencing

Videoconferencing can provide two way interactive teaching-learning facilities where the students can interact with highly qualified faculties from distant locations. This also reduces the costs involved in travel and energy. The visual contents should be used to furnish illustrations during the conferencing of the lecture, to permit pupils to experience the content through the avenues of sight and learning.

Virtual Classroom

Virtualizing is the creation of a three-dimensional, interactive model of a problem or dataset to find a virtual solution that will also work in the real world. Virtual reality also has the flexibility to be a tremendous aid for design in the areas of engineering and manufacturing, architecture and construction, biotechnology and nano pharmacology, chemistry and modeling molecules, medicine and bionics, the apparel sector, and the fine arts. Three-dimensional models of molecules and living structures may be fabricated and handled virtually. Electronics may be fabricated and tested absent creation of a physical prototype. Virtual modeling clay can be shaped into various forms for either aesthetic or practical purposes

Computer-artificially constructed objects and worlds should conform with reasonable accuracy to the tangible and other laws that shape such things and environments in the actual world. Some divergence might be relevant for surreal applications, but in case the difference is too great then the sense of believability is lost.

Some of the Virtual Classroom Equipments are;

1. E-D Wireless 3D Glasses for the PC
2. VirtualFX 3D TV Converter
3. 3DPlus 2D to 3D DVD Software
4. 3D Combine 2D to 3D Photo Software
5. 3D DVDs for your PC or TV
6. Long Range Viewing Equipment for Stereo Projection
7. InFocus DepthQ 3D Video Projector
8. 3D Glasses for Samsung and Mitsubishi Televisions
9. Vuzix - VR920 Head Mounted Display

Site

The satellite instructional television experiment was launched in our country in august 1975. The main Objective of the SITE programmes was to help people in their development endeavours. The major educational objective of INSAT television is to promote alternative approaches to education for children, youth and adults.

Insat

INSAT (Indian National Satellites) are a series of satellites projected and maintained by ISRO for multipurpose space applications. INSAT-3B, INSAT-3C are satellites in this series. The objective of the INSAT (Indian National Satellite - 1982) project was aimed at making the rural masses aware of the latest developments in the areas of agricultural productivity, health and hygiene.

Edusat

At present, using EDUSAT, networks for many user agencies like IGNOU, CEC/UGC, CIET/NCERT, AICTE, Blind People's Association

(BPA) or Blind school, Karnataka school network, VTU, YCMOU, Goa University, Amrita VRC, and Kerala/Tamil Nadu are operational for a total of about 1200 terminals or classrooms.

UGC Country wide Classroom

The University Grants Commission (UGC) was formally established only in November 1956 as a statutory body of the Government of India through an Act of Parliament for the coordination, determination and maintenance of standards of university education in India.

CLASS Project

A Pilot Project on Computer Literacy and Studies in Schools (CLASS) was initiated in 1984-85 in 248 selected Secondary/Higher secondary schools. The objective is to acquaint students and teachers with the wide range of computer applications and its potential as a learning medium. By the end of 1988-89 about 2600 schools had been covered. Sixty resource centers had been set up to train school teachers and provide support to the participating schools. Efforts have been made to start generation of indigenous software through NCERT, New Delhi. The project is jointly co-coordinated and supported by the Department of Electronics, the Department of Education, Computer Maintenance Corporation (CMC) and the NCERT.

Learning without Frontiers" (LWF)

It represents UNESCO's pro-active response to addressing the deep social and political problems that confront humanity as they relate to the role of learning in society. It views the processes of engaging in collaborative, multi channel and innovative learning as being critical for both the development of the individual and the building and linking of culturally diverse communities.

Conclusion

Reliable wireless service is has become an essential tool in both enhancing the education of electronic based teaching learning students as well as increasing operational productivity at SMART schools. Recent advances in Wi-Fi technology dramatically increase the range and reliability of Wi-Fi services by automatically focusing and directing signals over the fastest RF paths as the environment changes. A lot of modern classrooms are replacing classic white boards with "Smart boards". These smart boards are usually touch screen and are connected to a computer. This means that anything on the computer can be shown to an entire class relatively easily. Smart boards do require projectors and can be quite expensive; also environmental effects such as glare through windows can affect use. Everyone should show responsibility towards the LCD projector utility in their classrooms. To fulfill this objective we should educate our all teachers through this electronic technology. The management and authorities should initiates to use videos, documentary films and technology related magazines etc to build LCD projectors knowledge among teachers and develop the educational transactions.

References

1. Edwards, Julie-Ann, M. Hartnell and R. Martin (2002) Interactive Whiteboards: Some Lessons for the Classroom, Micro math, summer 2002, pp 30-33.
2. Gueissaz, Albert. (2002), New Tool, New Actors, New Decisions, European Journal of Education, Vol.37, No.1, p. 16-21.
3. Jo Towers (2007) Using video in teacher education, Canadian Journal of Learning and Technology. Volume 33, No.2 Spring 2007. pp. 54-58.
4. Mark Fischetti (November 2007) Two Technologies Shine, Scientific American, Inc: pp. 110–111
5. Nachimuthu, K. (2007), Mobile learning and Distance Education, Journal of Distance Education, University of Jammu, Kashmir, India, 2007, Vol. XII, No:1, pp. 33-39.
6. Solvie, Pamela A (2004) Digital Whiteboard: A Tool in Early Literacy Instruction. Reading Teacher, Vol. 57, No.5, pp.: 484–487.
7. Vijayakumari, G. et al., (2008), Quality issues and standards of E-content, Journal of Educational Technology, I-Manager Pub, Vol. 04, No. 03, Oct- Dec 2007, pp. 8-11.
8. Wu, C. H. and Lin, T. Y. (2000) Education terms: knowledge economy, knowledge management, Education information and research Journal, Vol.37, pp.100-101.

7

Use of Ict For Teaching Psychology in B.ed., Level

Introduction

ICT enriches the campus by incorporating its role well. This is present paper illustrates the use of ICT in various ways in teaching Psychology for students of B.Ed., Course. An attempt is made to analyze how technology could be best incorporated to the maximum benefit for the students. The purpose of this paper is to create awareness about the advantages of using ICT in a classroom and to illustrate how and when to use them effectively. This information can also be used in developing e-content or module for core paper II of Tamil Nadu Teachers Education University B.Ed., syllabus namely Psychology of Learning and Human development.

In the present educational scenario, ICT (Information and Communication Technology) is considered as an important tool in the entire educational system – curriculum, instruction and management. Class room instruction forms the basis for majority of educational processes. Hence it should aim at making the teaching learning process interesting, effective and goal oriented. In current scenario of a classroom there is a paradigm shift in the focus from teacher centered approach to child centered approach, autocratic classroom climate to democratic climate, lecture method to constructive activity, stress full learning to joyful learning, general learning to customized learning, teacher or instructor to facilitator. The advantages of using ICT are dealt with under the broad four categories, namely 1. As an aid-to augment the learning process 2. As an administrative tool-to effectively undertake other curricular transactions like administrating tests, evaluation, maintenance of records and many more. 3. As a subject per see to learn about ICT, thought it is only incidental in psychology class 4. As a medium of knowledge management – use a range of strategies and practices to create, identify, represent and distribute insights and experiences. The present study elaborate some ways and means to convert a traditional B.Ed., Psychology class room in to a smart class and mentions the advantages associated with it.

ICT as a Learning Process

In the B.Ed., Psychology syllabus prescribed by Tamil Nadu Teachers Education University there are ten units. The uses of multimedia are discussed here unit wise. In the first unit concepts about the various methods and branches of psychology can be easily illustrated by preparing power points by downloading pictures and images from the internet. Pictures, images or schemes are available in plenty for topics on S-R conditioning, Thorndike's puzzle box and Pavlov's classical conditioning. If the teacher is persistent enough she could get picture with beautiful animation too. The only problem the teacher face is the problem of plenty which could be easily overcome by the teacher developing a scanning eye with practice. Using visual perception it become easier for the students to distinguish conditioned stimulus from unconditioned stimulus, conditioned responds from unconditioned responds. Various website offer a large number of methods of psychology. For example a more look at the simple figure, the student is able to graphs the importance of the whole against the parts. The ice berg model of personality structure of Sigmund Freud's Psychoanalysis theory is well illustrated in many website. All that the teacher requires to do is to cut and paste these figures and make a presentation with notes of explanations. There are websites which offer Transactional Analysis well illustrated by schematic representations which rarely finds a place in many of the popular text books followed in B.Ed., colleges.

Another strategy to improve the understanding ability of the students is that different unit of Educational Psychology can be compared easily using a table with the Colum heading as' unit wise objective, concept, variation, main ideas and method adopted'. The topic of the units of Psychology namely "Nature of Educational Psychology, Human Growth and Development, Cognitive Development, Social, Emotional and Moral Development, Learning, Intelligence and Creativity, Motivation and Group Dynamics, Personality and Assessment, Mental Health and Hygiene and Guidance and Counseling from the row headings this table will provide the summary of all units the Educational Psychology. To add value to this table, pictures of the ten units can be pasted. It would serve as the ready beckoner for the exam oriented students.

Once the various approaches in psychology are made clear to the students by making use of ICT enabled instructional materials the major difficulties in getting through the other concepts in the minds of the students become easier for the teacher on one hand. On the other hand the students can easily go through this comprehensive table understand, appreciate, recall and recite. Since these are objectives most often tested in our present system of examination this in our present system of examination this would serve them the purpose. Similarly, the concept of Identical twins, Fraternal Twins, Mendelism, Sex determination in human being, the difference between positive reinforcement, negative reinforcement and punishment all these can be made easy by an ingenious teacher. One may argue that good books are available with excellent illustrations and figures. But most of the time a single book will not be giving the best illustration for all the concepts. But teacher can collect the best illustration, best images and best tables from the various freely downloadable sites and make her own presentation in a LCD projector. Over and above, already prepared PowerPoint's are also available for many of the topics which the classroom teacher can alter according to the needs of the students. In this context the uses of the free open source community based tool 'Moodle' cannot be overemphasized. This tool can be used effectively to speed up the process of learning among the students.

ICT- as an Administrative Tool

The uses of computer especially the packages MS office is tremendous in a classroom as an administrative tool. It is a boon to the classroom teacher. It is used for marking the attendance register, calculating the attendance percentage for issue of hall tickets, giving roll numbers or register numbers, preparation of question papers, preparation of key, entry of marks, maintaining rank card or progress report or a cumulative record.

ICT as a Subject

Even though it is in the purview of Engineering and technology students, the basic operations of the computer, knowledge about various tools, utilities and sites available are a must for any teacher. By using modern gadgets as tool in a classroom the students are bound to learn about them. Though incidental in the process learning psychology, the fundamental knowledge about ICT is an added advantage for students as well as teachers.

ICT as a Medium of Knowledge Management

We are in an information society. This does not mean that there is lot of data in the society. It means we have easier access to information today than ever before. Data is just a number or figure. With context defined a data becomes meaningful information. Knowledge management is employing various strategies and practices combining information gathered by technology or any other means with our past experiences and insights to attain the goal. Modern technology provides for knowledge management also. Internet, email, social websites like blog, twitter etc., help us to manager our knowledge.

Conclusion

The above cited illustrations of uses of ICT in a Psychology class are not exhaustive. The scope is very wide. Everything depends on the ingenuity and interest of the teacher. Suitable conditions should be ensured in schools and teacher education Institutes to implement effectively ICT integration. Only then we can achieve our target in converting our classrooms to totally smart classes.

References

1. Tamilnadu Teachers Education University, prescribed syllabus for Bachelor of Education (B.Ed.) Course 2011-12.
2. Computer Assisted Instruction (CAI) www. Wikieducator.org
3. Anna Martinkova, 2009, Inactive ICT in Education.
4. www. Smartclasonline.com
5. www. Learninghour.com
6. www. Educomp.planetvideo.com

8

Traditional Classroom Vs Flipped Classroom

Introduction

Flipped classroom is a form of blended learning in which students learn new content online by watching video lectures, usually at home, and what used to be homework is done in class with teachers offering more personalized guidance and interaction with students, instead of lecturing. Teachers can deliver this instruction by recording and narrating screen casts of work they do on their computers, creating videos of themselves teaching, or creating video lessons from trusted Internet sites. Students can watch the videos or screen casts as many times as they need to, enabling them to be more productive learners in the classroom. Since direct instruction is delivered outside the group learning space, teachers can then use in-class time to actively engage students in the learning process and provide them with individualized support. The traditional pattern of teaching has been to assign students to read textbooks and work on problem sets outside school, while listening to lectures and taking tests in class. In flip teaching, the students first study the topic by themselves, typically using video lessons prepared by the teacher. Flipping changes teachers from ''sage on the stage" to ''guide on the side", allows them to work with individuals or groups of students throughout the session. Key elements of the flipped classroom are to provide a mechanism to assess students understanding. Provide an opportunity for students to gain first exposure prior to class, an incentive to students to prepare for the class and also promote in-class activities that focus on higher level cognitive activities. By providing an opportunity for students to use their new factual knowledge while they have access to immediate feedback from peers and instructor, the flipped classroom helps student learn to correct misconceptions and organize their new knowledge such that it is more accessible for future use. More over the immediate feedback that occurs in the flipped classroom helps students recognize and think about their own growth in understanding.

Originally developed in 2000 by Wes Baker at Cedarville University in Cedarville, Ohio, the flipped classroom model has gained widespread traction across the country as a means to integrate computer and online resources with day-to-day coursework. The flipped classroom is a pedagogical model in which the typical lecture and homework elements of a course are reversed. Short video lectures are viewed by students at home before the class session, while in-class time is devoted to exercises, projects, or discussions. The video lecture is often seen as the key ingredient in the flipped approach, such lectures being either created by the instructor and posted online or selected from an online repository. While a pre recorded lecture could certainly be a podcast or other audio format, the ease with which video can be accessed and viewed today has made it so ubiquitous that the flipped model has come to be identified with it.

Flipped Classroom

Flipped classroom is a form of blended learning in which students learn new content online by watching video lectures, usually at home, and what used to be homework is done in class with teachers offering more personalized guidance and interaction with students, instead of lecturing. This is also known as backwards classroom, reverse instruction, flipping the classroom and reverse teaching.

The flipped classroom approach has been used for years in some disciplines, notably within the humanities. The students gain first-exposure learning prior to class and focus on the processing part of learning like synthesizing, analyzing and problem- solving in the class. To ensure that students do the preparation necessary for productive class time, an assignment-based model in which students produce work prior to class. The students receive productive feedback on the students' work.

Traditional Vs Flipped Teaching

The traditional pattern of teaching has been to assign students to read textbooks and work on problem sets outside school, while listening to lectures and taking tests in class. In flip teaching, the students first study the topic by themselves, typically using video lessons prepared by the teacher. In class, students apply the knowledge by solving problems and doing practical work. Complementary techniques include differentiated instruction and project-based learning.

Flipped classrooms free class time for hands-on work. Students learn by doing and asking questions. Students can help each other, a process that benefits both the advanced and less advanced learners. Flipping also changes the allocation of teacher engages with the students who ask questions-but those who don't ask tend to need the most attention. We refer to 'silent failers,' said one teacher, claiming that flipping allows her to target those who need the most help rather than the most confident. Flipping changes teachers from "sage on the stage" to "guide on the side", allows them to work with individuals or groups of students throughout the session.

Significance of Flipped Classroom

1. In a traditional lecture, students often try to capture what is being said at the instant the speaker says it. They cannot stop to reflect upon what is being said, and they may miss significant points because they are trying to transcribe the instructor's words.

2. By contrast, the use of video and other pre- recorded media puts lectures under the control of the students: they can watch, rewind, and fast-forward as needed.
3. Lectures that can be viewed more than once may also help those for whom English is not their first language. Devoting class time to application of concepts might give instructors a better opportunity to detect errors in thinking, particularly those that are widespread in a class.
4. At the same time, collaborative projects can encourage social interaction among students, making it easier for them to learn from one another and for those of varying skill levels to support their peers.
5. Concept engagement takes place in the classroom with the help of the instructor. Educational Technology and activity learning are two key components of the flipped classroom model.

How Does IT Work?

There is no single model for the flipped classroom the term is widely used to describe almost any class structure that provides pre-recorded lectures followed by in-class exercises. In one common model, students might view multiple lectures of five to seven minutes each. Online quizzes or activities can be interspersed to test what students have learned. Immediate quiz feedback and the ability to rerun lecture segments may help clarify points of confusion. Instructors might lead in class discussions or turn the classroom into a studio where students create, collaborate, and put into practice what they learned from the lectures they view outside class. As on-site experts, instructors suggest various approaches, clarify content, and monitor progress. They might organize students into an ad hoc workgroup to solve a problem that several are struggling to understand. Because this approach represents a comprehensive change in the class dynamic, some instructors have chosen to implement only a few elements of the flipped model or to flip only a few selected class sessions during a term.

Implications on Teaching and Learning

The flipped classroom constitutes a role change for instructors, who give up their front of the class position in favour of a more collaborative and cooperative contribution to the teaching process. There is a concomitant change in the role of students, many of who are used to being cast as passive participants in the education process, where instruction is served to them. Activities can be student-led, and communication among students can become the determining dynamic of a session devoted to learning through hands-on work. What the flip does particularly well is to bring about a distinctive shift in priorities from merely covering material to working toward mastery of it.

Key Elements of the Flipped Classroom

1. Provide an opportunity for students to gain first exposure prior to class.
2. Provide an incentive for students to prepare for the class.
3. Provide a mechanism to assess students understanding.
4. Provide in-class activities that focus on higher level cognitive activities.

Steps in Flipping the Classroom

1. Click on “Find and flip”.
2. Find YouTube videos for your lessons.
3. Click to select that video then click on flip this video.
4. Listed/unlisted.
5. Title/description.
6. Customize your video lesson.
7. Click on finish flip when you are done you can also preview it before saving it.
8. Share
9. Lesson starts.

Advantages

1. The expectation of spending time doing homework should be clear
2. Student can develop foundation of factual knowledge.

3. Students can understand facts and ideas in the context of a conceptual framework.
4. They can enrich their knowledge in ways that facilitate retrieval and application.
5. It saves time. Teacher may spend more time with students.

Conclusion

Meta-cognitive approach to instruction can help student learn to take control of their own learning by defining learning goals and monitoring their progress in achieving them. Although students thinking about the own learning is not an inherent part of the flipped classroom, the higher cognitive functions associated with class activity, accompanied by the ongoing peer/instructor interaction that typically accompanies them, can readily lead to the meta-cognition associated with deep learning.

References

1. Wesley, Baker.J (2000), The classroom flip: using web course management tools to become the guide by the side
2. Tucker, Bill (Winter 2012), "The Flipped Classroom", Education Next.
3. Pierce Richard, Fox Jeremy (20 Dec 2012), Vodcasts and active-learning exercises in a "flipped classroom" model of a renal pharmacotherapy module.
4. "Flipping the classroom", The Economist, 17 Sep 2011

9

Designing Learning Environment of Tomorrow

Introduction

Over the past decade, expert opinion and design recommendations for teacher professional development have moved steadily away from traditional workshop models and toward models that involve various types of professional collaboration among teachers. Whether expressed as the peer coaching model in the 70's and 80's, Professional Development Schools in the 80's through the present, or current day professional learning communities, collaboration is increasingly central to emerging models for professional development. Rigorous research on the impact of collaboration on teachers and teaching practices is just beginning to emerge. Literally no rigorous research is available directly linking collaborative professional development practices to improvements in student achievement or other student outcomes. Studies suggested that collaboration, in combination with specific configurations of professional development, may result in increased student learning and it is emphasized that authentic teaching learning environments will provide the fruitful results. The characteristics of learning environments are discussed in this article.

The influence of technology spreads its' wings to every sphere of life and life becomes so crucial and complicated. The educational principles and philosophies have changed drastically and online teaching learning becomes the order of the day. Unless we use this technology effectively the next generation will suffer with a number of confusion in utilizing the technology. Despite the intuitive appeal of authentic learning environments, and much anecdotal evidence that they are effective in promoting higher order learning, such complex learning environments appear to be used only rarely in higher education courses. Authentic learning designs have the potential to improve student engagement and educational outcomes. It is essential to provide an authentic environment for online teaching-learning which should facilitate students' learning in all the possible way.

Characteristics of a Situated Learning Environment

1. An authentic context that reflects the way the knowledge will be used in real life: In designing online learning environments with authentic contexts, it is not enough to simply provide suitable examples from real-world situations to illustrate the concept or issue being taught. The context needs to be all-embracing, to provide the purpose and motivation for learning, and to provide a sustained and complex learning environment that can be explored at length (e.g., Brown, Collins, & Duguid, 1989; Honebein, Duffy, & Fishman, 1993; Reeves & Reeves, 1997).

2. Authentic activities: The learning environment needs to provide ill-defined activities which have real-world relevance, and which present a single complex task to be completed over a sustained period of time, rather than a series of shorter disconnected examples (Bransford, Vye, Kinzer, & Risko, 1990; Brown, Collins, & Duguid, 1989; Reeves & Reeves, 1997; Lebow & Wager, 1994).

3. Access to expert performances and the modeling of processes: In order to provide expert performances, the online learning environment needs to provide access to expert thinking and the modeling of processes, access to learners in various levels of expertise, and access to the social periphery or the observation of real-life episodes as they occur (Collins, Brown, & Newman, 1989; Brown, Collins, & Duguid, 1989; Lave & Wenger,

1991). The facility of the World Wide Web to create global communities of learners who can interact readily via email, also enables opportunities for the sharing of narratives and stories.

4. Multiple roles and perspectives: In order for students to be able to investigate the learning environment from more than a single perspective, it is important to enable and encourage students to explore different perspectives on the topics from various points of view, and to 'criss cross' the learning environment repeatedly (e.g., Collins, Brown, & Newman, 1989; Honebein, Duffy, & Fishman, 1993; Spiro, Feltovich, Jacobson, & Coulson, 1991).

5. Collaborative construction of knowledge: The opportunity for users to collaborate is an important design element, particularly for students who may be learning at a distance. Consequently, tasks need to be addressed to a group rather than an individual, and appropriate means of communication need to be established. Collaboration can be encouraged through appropriate tasks and communication technology (e.g., discussion boards, chats, email, debates etc.) (e.g., Brown, Collins, & Duguid, 1989; Collins, Brown, & Newman, 1989; Hooper, 1992; Reeves & Reeves, 1997).

6. Reflection: In order to provide opportunities for students to reflect on their learning, the online learning environment needs to provide an authentic context and task, as described earlier, to enable meaningful reflection. It also needs to provide non linear organisation to enable students to readily return to any element of the site if desired, and the opportunity for learners to compare themselves with experts and other learners in varying stages of accomplishment (e.g., Boud, Keogh, & Walker, 1985; Kemmis, 1985; Collins & Brown, 1988).

7. Articulation: In order to produce a learning environment capable of providing opportunities for articulation, the tasks need to incorporate inherent—as opposed to constructed—opportunities to articulate, collaborative groups to enable articulation, and the public presentation of argument to enable defence of the position (e.g., Edelson, Pea, & Gomez, 1996; Collins, Brown, & Newman, 1989; Lave & Wenger, 1991).

8. Coaching and scaffolding: In order to accommodate a coaching and scaffolding role principally by the teacher (but also provided by other students), the online learning environments needs to provide collaborative learning, where more able partners can assist with scaffolding and coaching, as well as the means for the teacher to support learning via appropriate communication technologies (e.g., Collins, Brown, & Newman, 1989; Greenfield, 1984).

9. Authentic assessment: In order to provide integrated and authentic assessment of student learning, the online learning environment needs to provide: the opportunity for students to be effective performers with acquired knowledge, and to craft polished, performances or products in collaboration with others. It also requires the assessment to be seamlessly integrated with the activity, and to provide appropriate criteria for scoring varied products (e.g., Wiggins, 1993; Reeves & Okey, 1996; Linn, Baker, & Dunbar, 1991; Duchastel, 1997; Bain, 2003).

Authentic tasks

Authentic tasks are an integral component to situated learning environments, and it was felt important to investigate and describe their design more fully in order to explore their effective use in online learning environments. A literature review and study was undertaken where examples of online courses were investigated. The courses needed to use complex and sustained tasks that comprised an entire semester's work, so that in completing a single task, students would fulfil the requirements of the course. Such courses have been described in face-to-face and on-campus courses. Ten characteristics of authentic tasks were distilled from a review of papers on authentic learning environments from the literature and the characteristics were used to select cases for investigation:

1. Authentic tasks have real-world relevance: Activities match as nearly as possible the real world tasks of professionals in practice rather than decontextualised or classroom-based tasks (e.g., Brown, Collins, & Duguid, 1989; Jonassen, 1991; Lebow, 1993; Oliver & Omari, 1999; Cronin, 1993; Young, 1993; Winn, 1993; Resnick, 1987; Cognition and Technology Group at Vanderbilt, 1990a)

2. Authentic tasks are ill-defined, requiring students to define the tasks and sub-tasks needed to complete the activity: Problems inherent in the activities are ill-defined and open to multiple interpretations rather than easily solved by the application of existing algorithms. Learners must identify their own unique tasks and sub-tasks in order to complete the major task (e.g., Lebow & Wager, 1994; Bransford, Vye, Kinzer, & Risko, 1990; Cognition and

Technology Group at Vanderbilt, 1990a)

3. Authentic tasks comprise complex tasks to be investigated by students over a sustained period of time: Activities are completed in days, weeks and months rather than minutes or hours, requiring significant investment of time and intellectual resources (e.g., Bransford, Vye, Kinzer, & Risko, 1990; Lebow & Wager, 1994; Cognition and Technology Group at Vanderbilt, 1990b; Jonassen, 1991)

4. Authentic tasks provide the opportunity for students to examine the task from different perspectives, using a variety of resources: The task affords learners the opportunity to examine the problem from a variety of theoretical and practical perspectives, rather than a single perspective that learners must imitate to be successful. The use of a variety of resources rather than a limited number of preselected references requires students to detect relevant from irrelevant information (e.g., Young, 1993; Spiro, Vispoel, Schmitz, Samarapungavan, & Boeger, 1987; Bransford, Vye, Kinzer, & Risko, 1990; Cognition and Technology Group at Vanderbilt, 1990b)

5. Authentic tasks provide the opportunity to collaborate: Collaboration is integral to the task, both within the course and the real world, rather than achievable by an individual learner (e.g., Lebow & Wager, 1994; Young, 1993; Gordon, 1998).

6. Authentic tasks provide the opportunity to reflect: Activities need to enable learners to make choices and reflect on their learning both individually and socially (e.g., Young, 1993; Myers, 1993; Gordon, 1998).

7. Authentic tasks can be integrated and applied across different subject areas and lead beyond domain-specific outcomes: Activities encourage interdisciplinary perspectives and enable diverse roles and expertise rather than a single well-defined field or domain (e.g., Jonassen, 1991; Bransford, Sherwood, Hasselbring, Kinzer, & Williams, 1990).

8. Authentic tasks are seamlessly integrated with assessment: Assessment of activities is seamlessly integrated with the major task in a manner that reflects real world assessment, rather than separate artificial assessment removed from the nature of the task (e.g., Reeves & Okey, 1996; Young, 1995; Herrington & Herrington, 1998).

9. Authentic tasks create polished products valuable in their own right rather than as preparation for something else: Activities culminate in the creation of a whole product rather than an exercise or sub-step in preparation for something else (e.g., Barab, Squire, & Dueber, 2000; Gordon, 1998; Duchastel, 1997).

10. Authentic tasks allow competing solutions and a diversity of outcomes: Activities allow a range and diversity of outcomes open to multiple solutions of an original nature, rather than a single correct response obtained by the application of rules and procedures (e.g., Duchastel, 1997; Bottge & Hasselbring, 1993; Young & McNeese, 1993; Bransford, Vye, Kinzer, & Risko, 1990; Bransford, Sherwood, Hasselbring, Kinzer, & Williams, 1990). BEST (Beginning and Establishing Successful Teachers).

Conclusion

There are many teachers who employ authentic learning approaches in online courses. Widespread research at the practitioner level would add substantially to the knowledge we have about the advantages and disadvantages, affordances and limitations, and benefits and problems associated with authentic learning. The use of development research or design-based research studies would importantly contribute not only empirical knowledge about the veracity of the approach, but also design principles to inform theory and practice in education (Reeves, Herrington, & Oliver, 2004). Instructional designers and learning designers should perform an important role in this regard by considering the authentic principles of online learning thereby they can serve the student community in a better manner.

References

1. Bain, J.D. (2003). Slowing the pendulum: Should we preserve some aspects of instructivism? In P.Kommers & G. Richards (Eds.), World Conference on Educational Multimedia, Hypermedia and Telecommunications 2003 (pp. 1382-1388). Honolulu, Hawaii: AACE.
2. Barab, S.A., Squire, K.D., & Dueber, W. (2000). A co-evolutionary model for supporting the emergence of authenticity. Educational Technology Research and Development, 48(2), 37-62.
3. Gulikers, J.T., Bastiaens, T.J., & Martens, R.L. (2005). The surplus value of an authentic learning environment. Computers in Human Behaviour, 21, 509-521.
4. Herrington, A., & Herrington, J. (Eds.). (2006). Authentic learning environments in higher education. Hershey, PA: Information Science Publishing.
5. Herrington, J., & Herrington, A. (1998). Authentic assessment and multimedia: How university students respond to a model of authentic assessment. Higher Education Research and Development, 17(3), 305-322.
6. Kantor, R.J., Waddington, T., & Osgood, R.E. (2000). Fostering the suspension of disbelief: The role of authenticity in goal-based scenarios. Interactive Learning Environments, 8(3), 211-227.
7. Oliver, R., & Herrington, J. (2000). Using situated learning as a design strategy for Web-based learning. In B. Abbey (Ed.), Instructional and cognitive impacts of web-based education (pp. 178-191). Hershey, PA: Idea Group Publishing.

8. Reeves, T.C. (2000). Socially responsible educational research. Educational Technology, 40(6), 19- 28.
9. Reeves, T.C., Herrington, J., & Oliver, R. (2004). A development research agenda for online collaborative research. Educational Technology Research & Development, 52(4), 53-65.
10. Taylor, J.A. (2003). Managing staff development for online education: A situated learning model. Journal of Higher Education Policy and Management, 25(1).
11. Wiggins, G. (1993). Assessing student performance: Exploring the purpose and limits of testing. San Francisco: Jossey-Bass.
12. Winn, W. (1993). Instructional design and situated learning: Paradox or partnership. Educational Technology, 33(3), 16-21.

10

Preparing the Academy of Today for the Learner of Tomorrow

Introduction

Predicted to be America's first generation to exceed 100 million persons, the wave of Net Geners entering colleges and universities brings a blend of behaviors, attitudes, and expectations that creates opportunities—as well as challenges—for higher education. Opportunities arise from students' familiarity with technology, multitasking style, optimism, team orientation, diversity, and acceptance of authority. Challenges, on the other hand, include the shallowness of their reading and TV viewing habits, a comparative lack of critical thinking skills, naïve views on intellectual property and the authenticity of information found on the Internet, as well as high expectations combined with low satisfaction levels. Not surprisingly there is an increasing gap between most institutions' IT environments and the technologies the Net Gen uses. These factors lead, in turn, to the greatest challenge for higher education leaders, faculty, and staff—nearly all of whom belong to earlier generations: to understand the Net Generation learner and through this understanding provide the learning environments, services, and facilities needed to help these students achieve their potential.

Most institutions profess intense interest in the academic, social, and personal needs of their students. Yet, generational differences are not often used to gain a better understanding of students' behaviors, attitudes, and expectations. Change and adaptation within the academy proceed at a slow, deliberate pace. Planning is complicated because personal characteristics are not homogeneous within generational groupings. Unfortunately, the generational literature fails to predict the characteristics of future generations. Institutional leaders need to find ways to think about generations in designing campus and individual student initiatives, as well as to discern trends that will allow future-directed planning.

Generations and Technology

The technologies available as a generation matures influence their behaviors, attitudes, and expectations. People internalize the technologies that shape information access and use, as well as the ways they communicate. Matures (born 1946–1964) were exposed to large vacuum-tube radios, mechanical calculators, 78 rpm records, dial telephones, and party lines. Baby Boomers grew up with transistor radios, mainframe computers, 33? and 45 rpm records, and the touchtone telephone. Gen-Xers matured in the era of CDs, personal computers, and electronic mail. For the Next Generation, the prevailing technologies are MP3s, cell phones, and PDAs; they communicate via instant messaging, text messaging, and blogs. For each successive generation "technology is only technology if it was invented after they were born."

Technology has experienced its own series of generations. In computing, the nexus has shifted from the mainframe to the minicomputer to the personal computer, and now to mobile devices. In line with Moore's Law, computing and communication devices have radically decreased in size and increased in performance. Connectivity has experienced a similar transition across generations, from no connectivity to proprietary device-to-device cabling, to globally interconnected local area networks, and now to wireless.

Computers were initially developed as number crunching devices. The early emphasis on processing numbers, then words, has been joined by multimedia: graphics, images, video, sound, and interactive games. Prevalent among today's applications are interpersonal and group communication tools. The use of early computers was batch-processing-oriented and required programming skills and arcane commands. Today's graphical user interfaces and the Web make the operation of computers highly interactive and achievable by nearly anyone. The Internet has led to the kind of global village of information and communication.

Behaviors of the Net Generation are expressed through technologies to an extent not observed in previous generations. At one level, Net Geners are the beneficiaries of decades of technological development that preceded them; at another level, as students they use these technologies in new ways, and in so doing are redefining the landscape in higher education and perhaps beyond. To a great extent, the behaviors of the Net Gen are an enactment of the capabilities afforded by modern digital technologies.

According to a report from the Pew Internet & American Life Project, one in five of today's college students began using computers between the ages of 5 and 8; by the time they were 16 to 18, all of them used computers. Nationwide, nearly 90 percent of college students have gone online, compared with about 60 percent of the general population. Use of the Internet or campus networks is nearly universal in higher education. Eighty-five percent or more of college students own a computer, and nearly all of the rest have ready access to one. Sixty percent of college students regularly play computer or online games, and they are twice as likely to have downloaded music as the general population. The Net Generation students exhibit technology-related behaviors that may be unfamiliar to many in the academy: social networking, photo sharing, swarming, blogging, instant messaging, and text messaging. Four out of five students believe that Internet use has had a positive impact on their academic experience, and three out of four say they use the Internet for research more than they do the library.

Students are very familiar with the top online commercial sites such as Amazon. com and ambercrombie.com; they hold these sites to be the standard against which they judge colleges' online services. And, of all of the generational groups, the Net Generation is least satisfied with their higher education experience. Net Geners have access to affordable multifunctional devices (for example, cell phones equipped with digital cameras and Web browsers that can play digital audio and video recordings, as well as send and receive e-mail and text messages) that readily support their interpersonal communication needs and multitasking behaviors. Between classes, students bustle about with cell phones attached to their ears. Silberman described the prevalence of cell phones among Net Geners in Finland, and how cell phones' voice and short messaging capabilities allow them to move in synchronization "like schools of fish...on currents of whim." This behavior has since become well established in America, where it is known as social swarming or smart mobs.

Emerging Patterns

The mobility enabled by wireless communication, combined with an expanding class of wireless-equipped portable computers and PDAs, is leading to new instructional and social patterns. No longer do students need to go to a specific place, or even be seated, to use a computer. An array of multifunctional PDAs capable of wireless communication is allowing such devices to follow their users wherever they go, serving as "prosthetics for information, memory, or creativity." This is challenging the very definition of learning spaces because learning can now occur both in and out of the classroom, in both formal and informal settings, and by lone scholars or among groups. Net Gen students not only use technology heavily, they also trust it implicitly. They are as likely to get their news online as from a newspaper and conduct research through Google as visit a library. Their belief that anything accessible online should be free leads many to download or share music, movies, or software they have not purchased. The extent of this activity has surprised many institutions; campus networks often became saturated when students returned to school in the fall. In some cases this is followed by copyright violation notices from organizations such as the Recording Industry Association of America. The interactive and exploratory way the Net Generation uses technology is also a break with the past. The Net Gen approaches computers and other technologies as environments for communication, socialization, learning, and game playing, not as machines to be programmed. To be sure, today's students are avid users of Web, e-mail, telephones, and other IT resources; however, their rapid adoption of instant messaging, cell phones, blogs, wikis, social networking Web sites, and other resources that are not generally part of the core campus infrastructure leads to a host of new concerns. There is increased potential for incompatibilities between the technologies adopted by students and campus standards. The real opportunity lies in observing and talking to today's students to learn more about how they conceptualize and use these new tools. With this knowledge institutions can create contexts for technology use that enhance learning, improve student services, and enrich students' social lives.

Assessing the Generations in Online Learning

The Research Initiative for Teaching Effectiveness (RITE) at the University of Central Florida (UCF) regularly conducts formative and summative surveys of students' online learning experiences. These data become transformative because they are instrumental in modifying the organization, structure, and processes of our distributed learning initiative. We believe that both qualitative and quantitative research yield a more valid assessment of students in the online learning environment. When we ask respondents to complete objective statements followed by a reflective narrative, we obtain a more authentic characterization of their attitudes, beliefs, and behaviors. In the latest survey conducted at UCF, students used a series of 5-point Likert-scale questions to evaluate their online learning experience around two components previously identified through extensive numerical work. The first domain—learning engagement—encompassed six items where students indicated there:

? Overall satisfaction with online learning

? Ability to integrate technology into their education

? Ability to control their own learning

? Ability to study efficiently

? Ability to meet their educational objectives

? Willingness to take another online course

The second domain—interaction value—asked students to evaluate their online learning experience in regard to:

? Ease of interaction

? Amount of interaction with students

? Quality of interaction with students

? Amount of interaction with the instructor

? Quality of interaction with the instructor

Excellent Teaching

From our exploration of generational issues, an important question evolved: Can students distinguish characterizations of excellent teachers independent of generation, learning style, course modality, and technological sophistication? Data collected at UCF, with more than half a million student responses, suggest an answer. We have identified six characteristics that students attribute to the best faculty—characteristics that are independent of age, gender, and academic achievement. Interestingly, these characteristics correspond to the seven principles of good practice in undergraduate education and to the national study of student engagement. Although students' behaviors, attitudes, and expectations are generally shaped by their generation, what constitutes good teaching appears to be universal across these generations.

This seemingly paradoxical way in which students determine teaching excellence through the lens of their instructors clarifies how universities must accommodate students' needs, realizing that these needs are universal, yet greatly mediated by the Net Generation.

Conclusion

The Net Generation possesses sophisticated technological adaptability and a remarkable capacity to incorporate multitasking into day-to-day academic activities. However, there is also a growing discrepancy between institutional infrastructure and these students' personalized facility with information. Freeland described a corresponding trend emerging in higher education that he called practice-oriented education—the combination of liberal and professional studies. He foreshadowed the students' tendency to learn through bricolage and the university's reticence to respond: "After 1945 it [the academy] became steadily more open... but, as its clientele became more 'modern,' higher education became more traditional." As we move into the next decades, the resolution of that polarization compels colleges and universities to examine, and perhaps redesign, their strategic direction. Possibly, by studying how students interacted (politically, economically, culturally, socially, and technologically) with institutions' instructional climate in the past. From an instructional design perspective, we realize that knowing our students gives us many more options for engaging them in the learning process. The audacity with which the Net generation has burst on the academic scene has accelerated our need to understand its learning characteristics. A conundrum accompanies that solution, however: adaptation for the present generation may not be adequate for the next.

References

1. Neil Howe and William Strauss, Millennials Rising: The Next Greatest Generation (New York: Vintage Books, 2000).
2. Alan Kay quoted in Marc Prensky, Digital Game-Based Learning (New York: McGraw- Hill, 2000), p. 38.
3. Marshall McLuhan and Bruce R. Powers, The Global Village: Transformations in World Life and Media in the 21st Century (New York: Oxford University Press, 1999).
4. Steve Jones et al., "The Internet Goes to College: How Students Are Living in the Future with Today's Technology" (Washington, D.C.: Pew Internet & American Life Project, September 15, 2002), <http://www.pewinternet.org/reports/toc.asp?Report=71>.

11

Effectiveness of Edu-digital Skill among Higher Secondary Students

Introduction

The end of the 20th Century and beginning of the 21st Century witnessed very exciting changes, one of them being in the field of Information and Communication Technology. Educators have begin to realize that in the fast changing world of today, the students have to be prepared to cope intelligently with the social, economic and technological changes. The educational environment is changing rapidly as a consequence of ICT and will continue to change. Information and Communication Technologies (ICT) are electronic and/or computerized devices and associated human interactive materials that enable the user to employ them for a wide range of teaching and learning processes in addition to personal use. Around the world, educational systems are under increasing pressure to use the new information and communication technologies to teach students the knowledge and skills they need in the 21st Century. With the emerging new technologies, the teaching profession is evolving from an emphasis on teacher-centered, lecture-based instruction to student-centered, interactive learning environments.

The present study aims to find out the effectiveness of edu-digital skill among higher secondary students in Coimbatore District. A samples of 100 higher secondary students selected randomly were studied. A questionnaire method of survey was used to find out the effectiveness of edu-digital skill higher secondary students. The data were collected by using questionnaire as an instrument. Primary data were collected by conducting direct structured interview using questionnaire. All the respondents were asked the same questions in the same fashion and they were informed the purpose of study. t-test, Regression and correlation analysis were applied to test the hypotheses. The findings and observations are the result and outcome of the interpretations made during the study of analysis. The result found that edu-digital skill is positively correlated with higher secondary students.

Education, the foremost weapon for social reform, is now under the forces of change. Newly formed branches of knowledge and techniques of education facilitate the physical, mental and emotional development of the learners. Schools have an unavoidable role in acquainting the students with the nature of changing field of education and in making necessary changes in the instructional techniques. In the modern world of technological innovations, all educational institutions are trying to improve their quality in terms of facilities and academic outputs.

Scientific knowledge is exploding every day. Knowledge available to mankind today is emerging in the form of science and technology. There is no limit or end to the accumulation of scientific knowledge. It also satisfies the intellectual thirst of human beings. Science education is a bridge between science and education, using psychology. It links the most powerful concepts of science to the growing minds of children through active experimental pedagogy. Science education plays a prominent role in Indian educational system. It has, as its objective, the aim of providing individual learners a firm grasp of the concepts and processes of science as also to impart the ability to use scientific method of problem-solving. As a result of it, every aspect of human civilization has been influenced to a very great extent.

The present world is the world of science and technology. Science is the most inexhaustible storehouse of knowledge. Continuous advances in scientific and technological research have led to the growth and greater application of science in contemporary society. The purpose of science education is to give individuals a firm grasps of the concepts and processes of science and to develop scientific attitude, scientific reasoning, problem solving ability and scientific temper and to impart them the ability to use the scientific method to other situations in life. Hence science education has been included in school curriculum at all levels. It is however necessary that science teaching be impressive so as to inculcate its values in young minds.

The most striking innovation in the field of educational technology is the use of computers. Computer is included in the hardware approach of educational technology. It is one of the machines of automation in teaching and learning and is used for presenting individualized instruction. The main objective of teaching through computer is to provide the needed flexibility for individualizing the educational process. It meets the specific needs of the student in a way in which is almost impossible to do in a face-to face student-teacher relationship.

Computers should have a major role in the teaching-learning process. Computers have become an essential class room tool for the acquisition, analysis, presentation, and communication of data in ways that allow students to become active participants in research and learning. The computers offer students very important resources for learning concepts through simulations, graphics, sound, data manipulation and model building. Computers can improve scientific learning and facilitate communication of ideas and concepts.

There are three roles for computer in education. First, it functions as a tutor for students by presenting material, evaluating responses, and depending on the basis of the evaluation, deciding what to present next. Second, it is a tool that helps students perform calculations, analyze data, keep records, or write papers. Third, it functions as tutee by having told what to do through programming.

A computer program can be designed to create models for experimental purpose. Students, that particularly in higher education, have the benefits of using computer as a computational tool. They learn a programming language and write a program to solve some of their course work problems treating the computer as an aid in much the same way as a slide rule or a set of mathematical tables. Computers are capable of giving almost instant feedback, tirelessly, no matter how many learners 'get it wrong' and it is equally well known that human tutors have limited value when it comes to learners repeatedly getting things wrong.

Review of Literature

Anboucarassy (2010) studied the effectiveness of Multimedia in Teaching Biological Science to IX Standard students. The results of the study revealed that experiment group performed better than the control group due to the exposure of multimedia based learning. Thus multimedia helps the students to sustain their interest and also their retention power compared to the traditional method of teaching. The constant use of multimedia will make students understand more and achieve more in their academic achievement. Hence it was concluded that the multimedia approach is considered to be one of the best techniques for biology teaching at IX standard level.

Ponraj and Sivakumar (2010) studied the effectiveness of Computer-Assisted Instruction in Teaching Zoology in Relation to Learners' Personality. The major findings of the study indicated that achievement scores of experimental group students were higher than the control group students after the treatment.

Yusuf, Mudasiru and Afolabi, Adedeji (2010) investigated the effects of computer assisted instruction (CAI) on secondary school students' performance in biology. The findings of the study showed that the performance of students exposed to CAI either individually or cooperatively were better than their counterparts exposed to the conventional classroom instruction. Based on the research findings recommendations were made on the need to develop relevant CAI packages for teaching biology in Nigerian secondary schools.

Objectives

- To know the edu-digital skill among higher secondary students in Coimbatore district.

- To find out the effectiveness of Multimedia Programme in teaching among higher secondary students.

Methodology

Research may be termed as a systemic inquiry of verified knowledge, it is an organized deliberate effort to collect information, to analyze it, to put it together and finally to evaluate it. This research paper on methodology describes elaborately, the sample that was chosen, research design, objectives of the study, data collection, statistical techniques used for data and analysis.

Population

Population selected for this study was 100 higher secondary students in a selected school at Coimbatore District.

Attitude Scale towards Multimedia Programme

The attitude scale was used to measure the level of attitude towards Multimedia programme. The scale was constructed and validated by the investigator.

The attitude scale towards multimedia programme, consisting of 40 items, was designed by the investigator and was given to experienced teachers who were handling Computer Science in higher secondary schools, professors of Computer Science and Education and Educational psychologists. On the basis of the suggestions of above experts, some items were restructured and some were eliminated. Finally 25 items were selected for this test. The scale for measuring the higher secondary student's attitude towards multimedia programme in the study is of the Likert type. This scale has as many as 25 statements of which 20 are favorable towards multimedia programme and the remaining are unfavourable towards it.

Scoring

In the Likert type of scale, against each statement, five alternatives namely "Strongly agree", "Agree", "Undecided", "Disagree", and "Strongly disagree" are given. The subjects have to indicate their choice by putting a tick-mark (“) under one of the five columns against each statement.

For favorable statement weight age of 4,3,2,1 and 0 were given from strongly agree to strongly disagree in that order. For unfavourable statements the scoring was reversed. Thus the strongly agree response will get 0 and the strongly disagree response will get 4. Here the weight age of 0,1,2,3 and 4 were given from strongly agree to the strongly disagree in that order. Thus the score value lies between 0-100. The content validity of the tool was established based on the opinion given by the experts. The reliability of the tool was established by Split-Half method. It was found to be 0.83 which was significant.

Data Collection

Primary data, required for the present research work were collected by conducting direct interviews using questionnaire. All the respondents were given sufficient information about the Project work. These respondents were provided with the same questionnaires. They were also informed that they have to answer in the same fashion.

Hypothesis

- There is no significant difference between the pre and post test mean scores of experimental group students in their attitude towards multimedia programme.

Administration of retention test

The Attitude Scale towards Multimedia Programme was constructed and validated by the investigator and was administered to the subjects of the experimental group. The pre test scores on attitude towards multimedia programme were collected. Thus pre test and post test scores on attitude towards multimedia programme were computed for analysis.

Analysis and Interpretation

To find out the significance of the difference between the pre and post test mean scores of experimental group students in their attitude towards multimedia programme the ‘t’ test was used.

Table 1

Distribution of 't' value between the pre and post test mean scores of experimental group students in their attitude towards multimedia programme

Group	N	Mean	S.D	't' value	Level of Significant
Pre test	50	42.08	10.42	24.47	p<0.05
Post test	50	93.58	2.57		

There is no significant difference between the pre and post test mean scores of experimental group students in their attitude towards multimedia programme.

The obtained 't' value is statistically significant since it is greater than the table 't' value 1.96 at 0.05 level of significance. Hence the null hypothesis is rejected. It shows that there is significant difference between the pre and post test mean scores of experimental group students in their attitude towards multimedia programme. It is therefore concluded that the experimental group students show more favorable attitude towards multimedia programme in the post test than the pre test.

Table 2

Showing the Stepwise regression analysis predicting factors influencing effectiveness of edu-digital skill among higher secondary students and demographic variables

Sl.No	Step/Source	Unstandardized Coefficients Beta	Std. Error	Standardlized Coefficients Beta	Step t	P
1.	Gender	1.144	0.156	0.242	7.324	0.01
2.	Father education	1.254	0.359	0.163	3.495	0.01
3.	Mother education	2.615	0.462	0.361	5.661	0.01
4.	Monthly Income	2.175	0.402	0.280	5.410	0.01
5.	Father Occupation	1.022	0.513	0.137	1.992	0.01

* P < 0.01

Five variables viz Gender, Father Education, Mother Education, Monthly income and Father Occupation have significantly contributed for predicting the factors influencing effectiveness of edu-digital skill among higher secondary. The first variable Gender seems to be 7.324, Father education seems to be 3.495, Mother education seems to be 5.661, Monthly income seems to be 5.410 and Father occupation seems to be 1.992. The predictive value of these variables separately is 0.01.

Table 3

Showing the correlation between the effectiveness of edu-digital skill among higher secondary students and demographic variables

Factors	Effectiveness of edu-digital skill among higher secondary students
Gender	0.920**
Father education	0.849**
Mother education	0.914**
Monthly Income	0.880**
Father Occupation	0.855**

* Significant at 0.01 level

Effectiveness of edu-digital skill among higher secondary students is positively and significantly related to Gender (0.920), Father education (0.849), Mother education (0.914), Monthly income (0.880) and Father occupation (0.855). So, the direct relationship between the effectiveness of edu-digital skill among higher secondary students and selected demographic variables.

Conclusion

Computer and multimedia technology for education offers a number of benefits. They allow the teacher to structure and present the information with varying special effects to the students. They can also be used for the storage of audio-visual information of various types. Multimedia programmes provide a lot of benefits. The benefits for learners include flexibility of scheduled instruction at a location convenient to learners, reduced student time, assured progress in skill development, increased achievement and increased retention and continuous report to the learners of progress and accomplishments, specified performance criteria, good response and feedback.

The application of multimedia programme would definitely create a good learning environment in classroom, sustaining attention and motivating the students to learn effectively. The application of multimedia may create a congenial learning climate in schools and can bring real life situations. The investigator has chosen the topic for the present study in order to address the problem faced by teachers, teaching science, to foster involvement in new teaching approaches, to get a feeling of satisfaction through learning in the classroom, to create joyful learning environment and to stimulate active information processing for effective learning,

In a vast country like India, enormous work is now being done in the field of education, but it is still not possible to equip each and every school with all the facilities for teaching science. Secondary schools need high quality teaching aids. Multimedia, as a teaching aid, is very much effective with colour, sound and graphics, which are found in the audio, video movie media. Any diagram can be explained in detail with 3D effects, which helps the students understand clearly. The students can get a live vision of life's aspects and scientific factors. Multimedia includes use of computer.

The present study has found out that the multimedia programme is very effective in higher secondary level. As the present teaching-learning process in higher secondary classes is very rigid, time bound and outmoded, it was proposed to use multimedia programme.

As multimedia programme develops a favourable attitude towards multimedia programme, motivates the students to involve in the process of learning, attracts students' attention in learning, accelerates the students' understanding of concepts of subjects, increases the retention power and that it is highly suitable for all categories of students ranging from low to high achievers, it is suggested that this multimedia programme be widely adopted and implemented in educational institutions as computer laboratory facilities are available in all the schools and colleges to enable the learners to learn the subjects of their choice according to their own pace and ability. Learning through multimedia programme is very easy, understandable and comfortable to all categories of students for all types of subjects.

References

1. Anboucarassy, B. (2010). Effectiveness of Multimedia in Teaching Biological Science to IX Standard students. EDUTRACKS, 9(5): 37-38.
2. Dalacosta, K., Kamariotaki-Paparrigopoulou, M., Palyvos, J.A., & Spyrellis, N. (2009). Multimedia application with animated cartoons for teaching science in elementary education. Computers & Education, 52(4): 741-748. Retrieved March 20, 2010 http://www.linkinghub.elsevier.com/retrieve/pii/S036013 1508001905
3. Jian Hu, Hao Yu, Jun Shao, Zhiyong Li, Jiawei Wang & Yining Wang (2009). Effects of dental 3D multimedia system on the performance of junior dental students in preclinical practice: a report from China. Advances in Health Sciences Education, 14(1): 123–133. Retrieved March 20, 2010 http://www.springerlink.com/content/c0n8075m367131x1/
4. Kanmani, M., & Radha, M. (2009). "Effectiveness of CAI package in basic electronics teaching", Journal of All India Association for Educational Research, 21(1): 47-50.
5. Korakakis, G., Pavlatou, E.A., Palyvos, J. A., & Spyrellis N. (2009). 3D visualization types in multimedia applications for science learning: A case study for 8th grade students in Greece. Computers & Education, 52(2): 390-401. Retrieved March 21, 2010 http://portal.acm.org/citation.cfm?id=1480558
6. Ponraj, P., & Sivakumar, R. (2010). Computer-Assisted Instruction in Zoology in Relation to Learners' Personality. EDUTRACKS, 9(6): 34-37.
7. Yusuf, Mudasiru O., & Afolabi, Adedeji O. (2010). Effects of Computer AssistedIinstruction (CAI) on Secondary School students' performance in biology. TOJET: The Turkish Online Journal of Educational Technology, 9(1): 62-69. Retrieved March 21, 2010

12

Students Attitude Towards Audio-visual Aids used By the Teachers

Introduction

Audio Visual aids or Graphic aids are the form of visuals that are represented on plane surface. The subject matter areas that are represented in Audio Visual aids or Graphic aids are in an abridged and easily understandable form. They convey meaning mainly through relatively conventionalized symbols that are nearer to reality perceptually than verbal symbols. They secure the attention of the pupils by their attractive format and simplicity of layout. They convey the expected message by combination of visual and pictorial message made meaningful by suitable captions. Pictures and words blended in harmony deliver the required information. The idea conveyed by any graphic aid should be a single concept. The layout and words should not be complicated so as to puzzle the viewer and make him lose interest in the same. The statement "one good visual which can secure and maintain attention and educate the viewer in the desired area is worth a thousand words" is quite correct. Graphics could be truly considered as the shorthand language of the idea presented. The criteria for good graphics are that they should be simple, bold, legible, brief and have adequate margins. Graphics are only two-dimensional and should be carefully planned to offset the limitation. An Audio Visual aids or a graphic aid by eliminating non–essentials and by using bold symbolic representations with attractive portrayal should be able to create interest and secure the attention of the pupils. Since the message to be conveyed pertains to a single concept and hence brief, the viewer will not get perplexed on being exposed to the visual but will try to read and understand what is implied (visual and words).Audio Visual aids or a graphic aids could easily be prepared by and teacher using simple materials that are easily available and stored for future use. Making graphics should form an integral part of the teacher's preparation for teaching. Almost any material involving illustrations is basically graphic in nature. There can be an infinite variety of graphic materials. It is difficult to give a rigid list of these materials. The present study aims to find out the students attitude towards audio-visual aids used by the teachers in Coimbatore district. A samples of 100 respondents selected randomly were studied. An interview schedule method of survey was used to find out the attitude towards audio-visual aids. Primary data were collected by using a structured interview scheduled. All the respondents were asked the same questions in the same fashion and they were informed the purpose of study. ANOVA, t-test and regression analysis were applied to test the hypotheses. The data collected through questionnaires have been tabulated. The findings and observations are the result and outcome of the interpretations made during the study of analysis.

Graphs, Diagram, Posters, Maps, Comics, Cartoons, Charts, Globes, Display Board, Peg Boards, Hook and loop board, felt board, magnetic board, marker board, chalk board, bulletin board, models, Epidiascope, slight projector, over head projector (OHP), fields trips, excursion, exhibition, museums, radio, Television, Tape recorder, Video Caste Record VCR and Computers. By using audio visual materials in accessible process, materials givens objects changes in time, speed and space could easily be brought to the class. Audio visual aids can helps to imaginative teachers to solve the communication problems. It also helps to extend human experience. Use of audio visual aids results in greater acquisition of knowledge of facts and ensures longer retention of the information gained. It can provide effective substitutes for direct contact of students with environment-social and physical. It also adds an expected change in attitude and behaviour of the students. It can provide integrated experiences varying from abstract to concrete. It helps in to secure and retain to attention as well as develop the communication skills. It could be used to motivate and stimulate interest of students to gain further knowledge. Lastly, In a conventional teaching method teacher is the centre of attention and the primary sources of information.

An attitude is a mental state of readiness exerting directive or dynamic influence upon individual's response to all objects and situations with which it is related. Therefore if we can have some judgement about the attitude of an individual towards a specific thing or activity then we can have a fair idea as to whether the individual can be persuaded to participate in a particular thing or activity and whether he shall adopt it with interest and sincerity or not.

The attitude is the degree of positive or negative effect associated with some psychological objects namely institution, ideal, symbol, phrase, slogan, job or idea towards which people can differ with respect to positive or negative effect (Thurstone, 1946). The attitude is a dispositional readiness to respond to certain situations, persons, objects in a consistent manner which has been learnt and has become one's typical mode of response (Free Mann, 1950). According to Guild (1950) attitude is a tendency of individual to favour or not to favour some type of situation. The attitude may be considered as motivational perceptual states, which direct perceptions and predispose a person to act in accordance with perceptions (Allport, 1955). The attitudes are learnt pre-dispositions to respond positively to certain objects, situations, institutions, concepts or other persons (Aiken, 1979).

Review of Literature

Glee Harrah Cady and Pat Mc Gregor (2005) describe that "Internet is a network of network and the internet mostly connects network of computers".

Barry (2006) studied the relationship between student's perceptions of their science class room learning environment and attitude to four different scores of scientific information experiments, books, promote positive attitude towards experiment as a source of information, while less favorable environment promoted more positive attitude to the more authoritarian sources of information.

Schafer (2007) compared third and fourth grade students using ESS units with students using laid low science serious on classification skills, science achievements and science attitudes. No achievement or classification skill different were noted but ESS students had more favorable attitudes.

Williams (2008), "Attitude of high school pupils towards general science and its relationship with achievement and its subjects". In her study it is found to examine if there are any differences among the different groups of students such as boys and girls. Rural school pupil and Urban school pupils in respect of their achievement in science, attitude towards science and attitude forwards science education.

Martis Anandi (2009) developed the test on scientific attitudes (TOSA), taking the point of view that attitudes must be inferred from the behavior of students. They developed a multiple – choice format test. The developed behavioral definitions of eight attitudes: (1) critical mindedness, (2) suspended judgment (3) Respect for evidence (4) Honesty, (5) Objectivity, (6) Willingness to change opinions, (7) Open – mindedness and (8) Questioning attitude. The behavioral definitions to these eight attitudes were used to develop items.

Mohanty Ajay Kumar (2010) investigated attitudes towards education, critical thinking ability and specific effective behavious of (1) Students who had studied, the BSCS environmental models "Investing your Environment" (IYE), (2) Those students using one of BSCS biological science version and (3) Those studying models of Biology. He found that the ability of students who had experienced BSCS Biological science was significantly increased but no other differences were found among the students on any of the other variables.

Objective

- The present study attempts to investigate the attitude towards Audio-visual aids used by the teachers.

Methodology

Methodology is an important aspect of any research work. There are different methods followed at various stages of any investigation. The details of methods followed in this study such as selection of tools, sample frame, collection of data, and analysis of data are involved in this research paper. The study has been designed with the student's attitude towards Audio-visual aids used by the teacher's achievement. The major aim of the present study is to determine the student's Audio-visual aids used by the teacher.

Method of data collection

The investigator personally distributed the questionnaires to each member of the randomly selected sample. They were requested to answer the items in the booklet as per the instructions provided at the beginning of each questionnaire. Confidentiality of response was assured. The questionnaires were collected by the investigator from the employees. The responses were scored as per the scoring key of the respective questionnaire. Then the results were tabulated, analysed and discussed.

Sample

A sample is a finite number of observations (or) cases in a particular universe of which it is a pat (Good 1952). The investigator prepared a representative random sample of students studying VIII & IX standard in different schools at Coimbatore District. A sample of 100 students was finally selected.

Hypothesis

- Students have favorable attitude towards use of Audio Visual Aids in Coimbatore district school.

Nature of the Tool

The inventory contained general instruction for the students and information about bio data. In addition to that the specific instruction ware given to on the first page of the inventory. Space for collecting personal data like students name type of school, locality of the school, class, gender, community, religion, group, medium of instruction, birth order of the child and parental literacy.

Data Processing

The collected data were analysed using appropriate statistical techniques. The descriptive statistics such as mean and S.D, t-ratio were computed. In order to study the functional dependencies to indicate the likelihood of causal relationships between the variables, inferential statistical techniques of ANOVA and Percentage analysis were computed.

Analysis and Interpretation

Table 1: Showing Mean, SD and t-test for respondent about students attitude towards audio visual aids used by the teachers on the basis of type of the school.

Types of the school	N	Mean	SD	t-value	LS
Government	62	70.48	6.50	2.78	0.01
Private	38	73.30	10.33		

Hypothesis 1: Students do not differ in their student's attitude towards audio visual aids used by the teachers on the basis of types of the school.

The calculated t-value (2.78), which is significant at 0.01 level, confirms that there is a significant difference in student audio visual aids on the basis of type of the school. Hence the stated hypothesis is rejected. So government students have high level of audio visual aids than private school students.

Table 2: Showing Mean, SD and t-test for respondent about students attitude towards audio visual aids used by the teachers on the basis of locality of the school.

Locality of the school	N	Mean	SD	t-value	LS
Urban	74	72.24	8.11	1.07	NS
Rural	26	71.14	9.19		

Hypothesis 2: Students do not differ in their student's attitude towards audio visual aids used by the teachers on the basis of locality of the school.

The calculated t-value (1.07), which is not significant at 0.05 level, confirms that there is no significant difference in their audio visual aids on the basis of locality of the school. Hence the stated hypothesis is accepted.

Table 3: Showing Mean, SD and t-test for respondent about students attitude towards audio visual aids used by the teachers on the basis of Gender

Gender	N	Mean	SD	t-value	LS
Male	74	70.97	7.41	1.85	NS
Female	26	72.90	9.89		

Hypothesis 3: Students do not differ in their student's attitude towards audio visual aids used by the teachers on the basis of gender.

The calculated t-value (1.85), which is not significant at 0.05 level, confirms that there is no significant difference in their audio visual aids on the basis of gender. Hence the stated hypothesis is accepted.

Table 4: Showing Mean, SD and t-test for respondent about students attitude towards audio visual aids used by the teachers on the basis of group.

Group	N	Mean	SD	t-value	LS
Arts	56	69.19	5.37	5.58	0.01
Science	44	74.58	10.37		

Hypothesis 4: Students do not differ in their attitude towards audio visual aids used by the teachers on the basis of group.

The calculated t-value (5.58), which is significant at 0.01 level, confirms that there is a significant difference in student audio visual aids on the basis of group. Hence the stated hypothesis is rejected. So science students have high level of audio visual aids than art students.

Table 5: Showing Mean, SD and F-ratio for students attitude towards audio visual aids used by the teachers on the basis of medium of instruction

Medium of instruction	N	Mean	SD	F-ratio	LS
Hindi	50	70.20	9.64	6.49	0.01
English	30	71.75	4.19		
Kannada	20	75.00	11.60		
Total	100	71.78	8.58		

Hypothesis 5: Students do not differ in their attitude towards audio visual aids used by the teachers on the basis of medium of instruction.

The calculated F-ratio (6.49), which is not significant at 0.05 level, confirms that there is a significant difference in students attitude of audio visual aids on the basis of medium of instruction. Hence the stated hypothesis is rejected.

Table 6: Regression for student demographic characters and their attitude towards audio visual aids used by the teachers Model Summary

Model	R	R Square	Adjusted R Square	Std. Error of the Estimate
1	.436[a]	.190	.159	7.87

a. Predictors: (Constant)

Anova[b]

Model	Sum of Squares	df	Mean Square	F	Sig.
Regression	.4189.756	11	380.887	6.155	.000[a]
Residual	17821.724	88	61.881		
Total	22011.480	99			

a. Predictors: (Constant)

b. Dependent variable

Coefficients[a]

Model		B	Unstandardized Coefficients Std. Error	Standardized Coefficients Beta	t	Sig.
	Name of the	58.979	4.376		13.477	.000
School	Type of the	2.387	1.116	.139	2.139	.033**
	Locality of the	-1.000	1.005	-.058	-.995	.320
	Class	-.500	1.046	-.028	-.478	.633
	Gender	1.989	1.052	.115	1.891	.060
	Community	-1.365	.422	-.190	-3.233	.001**
	Religion	.757	.627	.068	1.208	.228
	Groups	5.255	.947	.306	5.548	.000**
	Medium of	2.183	.649	.191	3.365	.001**
instruction the child	Birth order of	-9.11	1.032	-.001	-.009	.993
literacy (Father)	Parental	-.143	1.003	-.008	-.143	.887
literacy (Mother)	Parental	-.585	.955	-.033	-.612	.541

a. Dependent Variable: Attitude towards Audi visual aids

** Significant at 0.01 level

According to the regression result it is known that the demographic variables are influenced nearly 19 per cent to measure their attitude towards audio visual aids. This is proved by the obtained r square value (0.19).

Further the calculated F-value (6.15) also significant at 0.01 level. It indicates that there is a significant influence between students demographic characters and their attitude towards audio visual aids.

Also from the obtained t- values the demographic variables such as type of school, community, group studied and medium of instructions the students studied are significant at 0.01 level. So it is concluded that there is a significant difference regarding attitude towards audio visual aids on the basis of these variables.

Conclusion

Audio Visual aids or graphic aids are the form of visuals that are represented on plane surface. The subject – matter areas that are represented in Audio Visual aids or graphic aids are in an abridged and easily understandable form. They convey meaning mainly through relatively conventionalized symbols that are nearer to reality perceptually than verbal symbols. They secure the attention of the pupils by their attractive format and simplicity of layout. They convey the expected message by combination of visual and pictorial message made meaningful by suitable captions. Pictures and words blended in harmony deliver the required information. The idea conveyed by any graphic aid should be a single concept. The layout and words should not be complicated so as to puzzle the viewer and make him lose interest in the same. The statement "one good visual which can secure and maintain attention and educate the viewer in the desired area is worth a thousand words" is quite correct. Graphics could be truly considered as the shorthand language of the idea presented. The criteria for good graphics are that they should be simple, bold, legible, brief and have adequate margins.

Findings of the study

1. Based on the results that students do not differ in their audio visual aids on the basis of types of the school
2. From the calculation that students do not differ in their audio visual aids on the basis of locality of the school
3. Based on the results that students do not differ in their audio visual aids on the basis of gender
4. Based on the results that students do not differ in their audio visual aids on the basis of group
5. From the analysis that students do not differ in their audio visual aids on the basis of medium of instruction

Discussion

Audio visual aids a process of inward journey to unravel the hidden potentialities of a being. It helps an individual to develop ones personality. A systematic approach of Audio visual aids helps an individual to see the all around development at physical, mental, intellectual and emotional level. The practice of use of audio visual aids makes an individual perfect. It removes the unwanted elements in the mind of the learner. It improves concentration and brings mental stability. Audio visual aids are an essential tool for students to achieve higher score in their studies as if improves concentration, memory and skills. The present study clearly indicates and recommends the students to use of audio visual aids as to develop positive attitude towards everything in their life which helps to excel themselves in their studies. The entire study concluded reveals that the use of audio visual aids has high achievement and expressed more favourable attitude.

Educational Implications

Audio-visual aids are very important and useful aids for teaching. As well as it creates high interest among the students to learn the subjects. So, the department of education shall take a steps to implement the latest audio-visual aids to all the school and colleges for teaching purpose. For self-learning, these type of aids are very helpful to the students. Also students are very much interested in using latest technologies such as computers and internet. In internet lot of facilities are there to learn new information with visual appearance. From that students are also get more interest to use that.In the case of teaching, in older days teachers follow interactive methods and oral demonstration. But these are not creating much interest. In order to create interest and attention audio-visual aids are highly useful. So, the concerned educational institution tries to provide these facilities. So that teachers and students get benefited.

Suggestions

The following suggestions are arrived from the research findings. Research found that use of audio visual aids will contribute more in students achievement. Also the result reveals that use of audio visual aids increases the memory power, concentration. Further it sharpens the intelligence. Apart from that it reduces misconception in learning. Further due to use of audio visual aids the sensory expression would be more exercised. So, the present research suggested that in all schools and colleges, the students advised to use of audio visual aids compulsory. The education department forms a rule for that and advises the educational institutions make a step to establish separate infrastructure for this one. Also the Government take a step to use audio visual aids effectively students in their academic. This will definitely help the students to be a good learner imbibing the concepts.

Conclusion

The present study attempted to identify the students attitude towards audio-visual aids used by the teachers. For that the researcher framed some objectives. On the basis of objectives, a questionnaire is framed. After framing the questionnaire, these are circulated to the selected samples. 100 samples were selected randomly. The responses were collected and coded using computerised. To test the hypotheses and characteristics of the data, some standard statistical tools were used. The statistical tools such as t-test, F-ratio and correlation were used. From the analysis the result concluded that the students have positive attitude towards audio-visual aids used by the teachers.

References

1. Glee Harrah Cady and Pat Mc Gregor (2005) "Internet is a network of network and the internet mostly connects network of computers". Journal of research in science teaching.
2. Barry (2006) "Relationship between students perceptions of their science class room learning environment and attitude", Journal of Educational Research.
3. Schafer (2007) vargo students science attitudes and self concept in science as a function of rose specific pupil/teacher interpersonal compatibility", San Francisco, California, National association for research in science teaching.
4. Williams (2008), "Attitude of high school pupils towards general science and its relationship with achievement and its subjects". Journal Community and Guidance.
5. Martis Anandi (2009), in test on scientific attitudes (TOSA), taking the point of view that attitudes must be inferred from the behavior of students, Journal of All India Association for Educational Research, Vol.17, Nos. 1 & 2, March & June.
6. Mohanty Ajay Kumar (2010), Attitudes towards education, critical thinking ability and specific effective behavious, Journal of all India Association for Educational Research, Vol.14, Nos.3 & 4.

13

Learning Styles of Higher Secondary Students in Biological Science

Introduction

Learning style is a hypothetical contract that has been developed to explain the process of mediation between stimuli and response. Learning style as on integral concept that bridges the personality cognitive dimensions of the individuals. The learning styles are synonymous. He defines learning styles as the course of learning. Laycock (1978) describes learning styles as an individual characteristic way of responding to certain variable in the instructional environment. In simplest terms, a students learning style is the peculiar way with which he learns best. The present study aims to find out the learning styles of higher secondary students in biological science in Villupuram District. A samples of 100 respondents selected randomly were studied. A questionnaire method of survey was used to find out the learning styles of higher secondary students in biological science. The data were collected by using questionnaire as an instrument. Primary data were collected by conducting direct structured interview using questionnaire. All the respondents were asked the same questions in the same fashion and they were informed the purpose of study. Regression and correlation analysis were applied to test the hypotheses. The data collected through questionnaires have been tabulated. The findings and observations are the result and outcome of the interpretations made during the study of analysis. The result found that average learning styles of higher secondary students in biological science in Villupuram District.

The act or experience of one that learns. Knowledge or skill acquired by instruction or study. Modification of a behavioral tendency by experience (as exposure to conditioning). Adapted from How Learning Works by Ambrose et al.: an engagingly written, evidence-based text, well-illustrated by practical examples, and a book well worth your time, as a TA and as a student.

As teachers, our goal is to encourage learning in our classrooms. But what is learning, and what principles or factors affect how our students learn? In this section, we provide you with the very basics of what learning are, how and when it occurs, and how to structure your lessons to maximize student learning. There are three components to the definition of Learning:

1. **"Learning is a process, not a product."** Exam scores and term papers are measures of learning, but they are not the process of learning itself.
2. **"Learning is a change in knowledge, beliefs, behaviors or attitudes."** This change requires time, particularly when one is dealing with changes to core beliefs, behaviors, and attitudes. Don't interpret a lack of sea change in your students' beliefs or attitudes immediately following a lesson as a lack of learning on their part, but instead, consider that such a change will take time – perhaps a few weeks, perhaps until the end of the term, or even longer.
3. **"Learning is not something done to students, but something that students themselves do."** If you have ever carefully planned a lesson, only to find that your students just didn't "get it," consider that your lesson should be designed not just to impart knowledge but also to lead students through the process of their own learning.

Learning is the process by which one acquires, ingests, and stores or accepts information. Our experiences with learned information compose our bodies of knowledge. Learning is a process unique to each individual. Some learn quickly, scanning the information and mastering the concept or skill seemingly effortlessly. Others stumble while processing information, taking longer to grasp the concept or requiring numerous exposures over a sustained period of time. Some individuals store the information they've learned indefinitely, cementing it in their memories. Others find that the information they've learned slips away rapidly. Some learn best through text, others through practice, some through hearing. Learning styles are as unique and varied as our personalities. Learning is a lifelong endeavor. As long as one remains engaged in life, learning does not cease.

Until recently most people took learning styles for granted and left them to instinct. Realization that studying how learning should come before everything else is spreading in the world of education skill in this field can multiply efficiency. The use of higher level work skills can bring improvement in almost all fields. Improvement in athletic field and industrial productivity has been achieved in the way. Everyone is familiar with the difference in output of a self-taught typist who uses one finger of each hand and an expert who was taught the tough system. Other experiments has shown that the level of performance on such tasks as card sorting, pitch discrimination and puzzle solving is affected by the method employed and the limit to performance might be improved of better work was used.

These findings on effects of work methods on levels of performance led to the significant theoretical contribution to theories regarding the causes of individual difference in competence. It was long assumed that these differences were primarily due to two factors. (1) Learning and (2) Amount of training in a task. Dr. Seashare after studying may findings on effects of work method, concluded that method of work was a third variable in instruction. It is found that new levels in achievement are possible by improving the learning styles.

Both in common speech and educational literature the word "Read" is used to designate a wide variety of learned activities from the socially undesirable to the highly ethnical, form bodily skill, such as walking to mental activities such as learning of critical thinking and from specified abilities to generalized attitudes. The meaning of learning includes the ideal of facility in the performance of an act, combined with a persisting inclination towards the repetition of the act.

As Bagley has said "To teach a child to study effectively is to do that most valuable thing that could be done to help him adjust himself to any environment of modern civilized life into which they live. In 1917 strays and Newsworthy declared "Many teachers have taught subjects, but not how to study subjects, the latter is more important". H.R. Bhatia says, "unless opportunities for doing and respecting things are afforded to children it is futile to expect them to form habits". Sevmors and exhortations may help children to acquire normal vocabulary but not normal character. Percepta in the formation of learning unless children are afforded actual practice in those modes behaviour.

Review of Literature

Mary Lou Koran, John J. Koran (2006), conducted a study "Interaction of Learner aptitudes with question packing in learning from prose, he suggested that, in some cases, reduction in certain information Processing requirements may actually be an important prerequisite to affective utilization of other aptitudes (learning).

The over-all means used in the analysis are presented, both low and high aptitude students in "favourable" classrooms had higher achievements scores than the two groups in 'unfavourable' classroom. This contexts effect was present to some extent in both third and fourth grade class room aptitude, third grade students. It appears that being in a classroom with many high-aptitude students is beneficial for low-aptitude students and some high-aptitude students as well".

K.S Kahlon and Vinod Uppalo, (2007) studied on "women's aptitude and achievement in Relation to achievement motivation.

The Result of the present investigation fully support the hypotheses on the basis of which the study had been undertaken.

1. There is significant, but imperfect relationship between aptitude (learning style) and academic achievement.
2. Discrepancy between aptitude (Learning style) and achievement bears no relationship with ability.
3. Discrepancy between aptitude (Learning Style) and achievement bears significant relationship with academic achievement.
4. Discrepancy between aptitude and achievement bears significant relationship with achievement motivation. That is, high achievement motivation goes with positive discrepancy where as low achievement motivation accounts for negative discrepancy"

Robert B. Burnes (2012) conducted a study on "The Relation of Aptitudes of Learning at different Points in the time during Instruction: The result of this study suggested that some aptitude-learning relations are not stable over time and that his instability is exhibited in different aptitudes being required at different points in time during instruction. These findings supported most of the Junior evidence examining aptitude correlates at different stages of learning and did not support the assumption made in ATI Research that aptitudes relate equally to learning for the during of treatment"

Moraddwaj Varma (2013) conducted a study on "Comparative achievement in science of Tharu Tribals and other at high school level. He found, that the achievement of Tharu tribals is lower than that of the non-tharus in all the three science subjects were significant at .01 level."

In **Jamur (2013)** made a study in Patna in relationship between study habits and achievement. His study showed a correlation of 0.51 between study habits and achievement of students and a correlation of 0.144 between study habits and intelligence.

Objectives

1. To study the higher secondary learning styles in Biological science.

2. To know the higher secondary different methods learning styles in Biological science.
3. To find out the higher secondary factors learning styles in Biological science.

Methodology

The methodology adopted for the study is explained in detail. The sampling technique, size of the sample, variables of the study, description of the tool used and administration of tool are elaborated.

Sample

The sample selected for the present study is 100 higher secondary students in Villupuram district. Random sampling technique was used for the selection of sample.

Data Collection

Primary data, required for the present research work were collected by conducting direct interviews using questionnaire. All the respondents were given sufficient information about the Project work. These respondents were provided with the same questionnaires. They were also informed that they have to answer in the same fashion.

Tools used in the Study

SOLAT Tool of learning style D. Venketraman (1986) consists of 25 items. The learning style comprises 5 categories.

1. Verbal (1 to 5 items)
2. Content preference (6 to 10 items)
3. Class preference (11 to 15 items)
4. Learning preference (16 to 20 items)
5. Interest (20 to 25 items)

Scoring Procedure

1. The maximum score that a student obtains is 50 the minimum score that a student gain is 25.

2. Each item has two alternatives. If the student chooses the First alternative one mark is given. If the student chooses Second alternative the student it secures 2 marks. The first alternative of an item indicates the use of Right hemisphere of the brain and the second alternative of an item indicates the use of left hemisphere of the brain.

Tool validity and reliability

The main attributes needed to be considered regarding a good tool are validity and reliability.

Validity: A measuring instrument is said to be valid if it measures what it purpose to measure. Validity may be defined as the extent to which an instrument or a test does the job derived of it.

The kind of validity and the extent or degrees to which it should be established are the major consideration while establishing validity.

In the present study the researcher found out the content validity.

Content validity gives the logical evidence that the content of the items of a test is suitable for the purpose for which the test is designed and used. Content validity is established is 0.549.

Reliability

The efficiency of measuring the different items are called on aspect of reliability. Reliability determined test-retest method and it is found to be validity of the tool is (0.82).

Hypothesis

1. The level of learning styles among higher secondary students on the basis of their demographic variables.
2. The level of different method learning styles among higher secondary students on the basis of their demographic variables.
3. The level of factors learning styles among higher secondary students on the basis of their demographic variables.

Analysis and Interpretation

Table 1

Showing the Stepwise regression analysis predicting learning styles among higher secondary students and demographic variables

Sl.No	Step/Source	Unstandardized Coefficients Beta	std. Error	Standardized Coefficient Beta	Step t	P
1.	Gender	1.342	0.343	1.245	5.432	0.01
2.	Locality	1.224	0.392	0.269	6.641	0.01
3.	Family Income	1.924	0.549	0.149	4.142	0.01
4.	Father Education	2.334	0.667	0.108	5.339	0.01

* P < 0.01

Four variables viz Gender, Locality, Family income and Father Education have significantly contributed for predicting the learning styles among higher secondary students. The Gender seems to be 5.432, Locality seems to be 6.641, Family income seems to be 4.142 and Father education seems to be 5.339. The predictive value of these variables separately is 0.01.

Table 2

Showing the Stepwise regression analysis predicting different method learning styles and demographic variables

Sl.No	Step/Source	Unstandardized Coefficients Beta	std. Error	Standardized Coefficient Beta	Step t	P
1.	Type of Family	1.133	0.505	0.434	2.246	0.01
2.	Religion	1.248	0.466	0.782	2.677	0.01
3.	Community	1.792	0.683	0.646	2.625	0.01
4.	Birth Place	2.338	0.670	0.954	3.490	0.01

* P < 0.01

Four variables viz Type of family, Religion, Community and Birth place have significantly contributed for predicting the method learning styles. The first variable Type of family seems to be 2.246, Religion seems to be 2.677, Community seems to be 2.625 and Birth place seems to be 3.490. The predictive value of these variables separately is 0.01.

Table 3

Showing the Stepwise regression analysis predicting factors learning styles among higher secondary students and demographic variables

Sl.No	Step/Source	Unstandardized Coefficients Beta	std. Error	Standardized Coefficient Beta	Step t	P
1.	Gender	5.195	1.030	0.824	5.041	0.01
2.	Family Monthly Income	1.809	0.451	0.443	4.016	0.01

* P < 0.01

Two variables viz Gender and Family Monthly Income have significantly contributed for predicting the factors learning styles among higher secondary. The first variable Gender seems to be 5.195, when paired with the second variable Family monthly income is 1.809. The predictive value of these variables separately is 0.01.

Table 4

Showing the correlation between the learning styles of higher secondary students and demographic variables

Factors	Learning styles of higher secondary students
Gender	0.579*
Locality	0.782**
Family Income	0.591*
Father Education	0.572*
Type of Family	0.824**

* Significant at 0.01 level ** Significant at 0.05 level

Learning styles of higher secondary students is positively and significantly related to Gender (0.579), Locality (0.782), Family Income (0.591), Father Education (0.572) and Type of family (0.824). So the direct relationship between the Learning styles of higher secondary students and demographic variables.

Conclusion

The present study aims to find out the higher secondary students learning styles. The researcher framed objectives and hypotheses on the basis of the above context. The research was carried out in

100 samples based randomly. A questionnaire constructed by R was used to collect the relevant data. After collecting the data they were analyzed using statistical tools such as Regression and Correlation analysis. The result concluded that students have average level of learning styles at Higher Secondary level in Biological science in Villupuram District.

References

1. Hammet Gandhi, H. & Varma, M. (2008). Elucidating Mathematical problem solving through met cognition. Journal of Indian Education, 30(3).
2. Kaholan & Vinod uppal, (2007) Womens attitude and achievement in relation to achievement motivation, Journal of Education and Psychology, Vol. xxxviii, No 3: 198-201.
3. Live, Carl (2008) Formative Assessment Pre- Test to Identify College students' Prior Knowledge, Misconceptions and Learning Difficulties in Biology. International Journals of Science and Mathematics Vol.4.
4. LongDon, Bernard (2013) Genetics - Are there inherent learning difficulties?
5. Lovelace, M. K. (2005). Meta-Analysis of Experimental Research Based on the Dunn and Dunn Model. Journal of Educational Research, 98(3), 176-183.
6. Malini, Sujatha (2006) The Attitude of special and Normal School Teachers towards children with Disabilities.
7. Mary Lou Koran, John J. Koran (2006) Individual and teacher/ class effects in aptitude treatment studies, American Educational Research Journal, Vol.17, No.3: 291-302.
8. Mary Lou Koran, John J. Koran (2006) Individual and teacher/ class effects in aptitude treatment studies, American Educational Research Journal, Vol.17, No.3: 291-302.
9. Robert B. Burns, (2012) The relation of aptitude to learning at different points in the time during instruction, Journal of Educational Psychology, Vol. 72, No.6: 705-789.

14

Transitive Cloud Computing for Teaching learning Process

Introduction

This paper is an introduction to the terms, characteristics and services associated with internet-based computing, commonly referred to as cloud computing. The primary business service models being deployed, such as software, platform and infrastructure as a service - and common deployment models employed by service providers and users to use and maintain the cloud services, such as private, public, community, and hybrid clouds are discussed. Cloud computing is not something that suddenly appeared overnight: in some form it may trace back into our time when computer system remotely shared computing resources and applications. Some of the notable challenges associated with Cloud computing is that it not delivers more services in the cloud, it also can provide opportunities, if resolved with due care and attention in the planning. Lack of standard-clouds have documented inter faces; however, no standards are associated with these, and thus it is unlikely that most clouds will be interoperable. The open grid forum is developing an open Cloud computing interface to resolve this issue and the open cloud consortium is working on Cloud computing standards and practices. An important function of the Cloud is that it automatically saves content, making it impossible to lose or delete any valuable material. This means that even if a computer crashes, all documents and content will remain safe and accessible in the cloud. Any data stored in the Cloud can easily be accessed from almost any device including mobile devices such as phones or tablets. With the availability of content online, it is no longer necessary for teachers to spend time and resources printing or copying lengthy documents or lesson plans. Now, students are able to access homework assignments, lesson notes, and other materials through online.

The term "cloud" as used in this white paper, appears to have its origin in network diagrams that represented the internet, or various part of it, as schematic clouds. "Cloud computing" was coined when applications and services were moved into the internet "Cloud". Cloud computing is not something that suddenly that appeared overnight: in some form it may be traced back into our time when computer system remotely shared computing resources and applications. Cloud computing refers to many different types of services and applications being delivered in the internet cloud and the fact that in many cases the device used to access these services and applications do not require any special applications.

How Cloud Computing is Used in Education?

Cloud computing take education to the next level. There is no surprise that cloud computing education is a necessary tool for many companies and even schools. In this type of calculation, this should not be confused with others such as grid computing, utility computing or autonomic computing. Even if you are not completely familiar with cloud computing, you are certainly in touch with it on a regular basis, such as in use in computer applications like Skype. The interesting part about cloud computing is that entire systems can be set on a rental basis. Rather than more commonly owned tools to be engaged, it is true that cloud computation is another form of resource where teaching can take place. Most people use it to teach through social networking sites such as Face book and MySpace, email systems like Hotmail, gmail etc....

Cloud Computing is an umbrella term used to describe Cloud Computing services that are hosted on a network (typically the internet) and used by the PCs (or other devices) without mentioning specific servers or systems for teaching.

Characteristics of Cloud Computing

Shared infrastructure – uses a virtualized software model which enables the sharing of physical services, storage and networking capabilities. The cloud infrastructure regardless of deployment model seeks to make the most of the available infrastructure across a number of users.

Dynamic provisioning – It allows for the provision of service based on current demand requirements. This is done automatically using software automations enabling the expansions and contraction of service capability as needed. This dynamic needs to be done while maintaining the high level of reliability and security.

Network access – needs to be accessed across the internet from a broad range of devices such as PCs, laptops and mobile devices, using standard based APIs (For e.g., ones is based on http). Deployments of services in the cloud include everything from business applications to the latest applications on the newest smart phones.

Managed Metering – uses metering for managing and optimizing the services and to provide reporting and billing information. In this way consumers are billed for services according to how much they actually use during the billing period.

Service Models

Software as a service (SaaS) - consumers purchase the ability to access and use an application or service that is posted in the cloud.

Platform as a service (PaaS) - consumers purchase access to the platforms, enabling them to deploy their own software and applications in the cloud.

Infrastructure as a services(IaaS) - consumers control and manage their systems in terms of the operating system, applications, storage, and network connectivity, but do not themselves control the cloud infrastructure.

Deployment Models

Deploying Cloud computing can differ depending on requirements, and the following four development models have been identified:

Private cloud-the cloud infrastructure has been deployed, and is maintained and operated for a specific organization. The operation may be in-house or with the third party on the premises.

Community cloud- the cloud infrastructure is shared among the number of organizations with similar interest and requirements.

Public cloud- the cloud infrastructure is available to the public on the commercial basis by a cloud service provider.

Hybrid cloud- the cloud infrastructure consists of a number of clouds of any type, but the clouds have the ability through their interfaces to allow their data and/or applications to be moved from one cloud to another.

Advantages

1. **Back Up:** An important function of the Cloud is that it automatically saves content, making it impossible to lose or delete any valuable material. This means that even if a computer crashes, all documents and content will remain safe, saved, and accessible in the cloud.
2. **Storage:** The Cloud allows its users to store almost all types of content and data including music, documents, eBooks, applications, photos, and much more.
    1. **Accessibility:** Any data stored in the Cloud can easily be accessed from almost any device including mobile devices such as phones or tablets.
    2. **Collaboration:** Because the Cloud allows multiple users to work on and edit documents at the same time, it enables effortless sharing and transmission of ideas. With this feature, group projects and or collaborative lesson plans can be optimized for both teachers and students.

3. **Resource and Time Conscious:** With the availability of content online, it is no longer necessary for teachers to spend time and resources printing or copying lengthy documents or lesson plans. Now, students are able to access homework assignments, lesson notes, and other study materials online.
4. **Assignments:** I love the Cloud to allow teachers to post assignments online. Students are able to access these assignments, complete them, and save them in a folder to be reviewed later.

Benefits

1. Cost savings
2. Scalability or flexibility
3. Reliability
4. Maintenance
5. Mobile accessible

Challenges

Security and privacy - perhaps two of the more "hot button" issues surrounding Cloud computing relate to storing and securing data, and monitoring the use of the cloud by the service providers. These issues are generally attributed to slowing the deployment of cloud services.

Lack of standards - Clouds have documented inter faces; however, no standards are associated with these, and thus it is unlikely that most clouds will be interoperable. The open grid forum is developing an open Cloud computing interface to resolve this issue and the open cloud consortium is working on Cloud computing standards and practices. The findings of these groups will need to mature, but it is not known whether they will address the needs of the people deploying the services and the specific interfaces these services need.

Continuously evolving - user requirements are continuously evolving, as are the requirements for interfaces, networking and storage. This means that a "cloud," especially a public one, does not remain static and is also continuously evolving.

Conclusion

As cloud computing is achieving increased popularity, concerns are being voiced about the security issues introduced through adoption of this new model· The effectiveness and efficiency of traditional protection mechanisms are being reconsidered as the characteristics of this innovative deployment model can differ widely from those of traditional architectures. Any data stored in the Cloud can easily be accessed from almost any device including mobile devices such as phones or tablets. With the availability of content online, it is no longer necessary for teachers to spend time and resources printing or copying lengthy documents or lesson plans. Now, students are able to access homework assignments, lesson notes, and other materials through online.

References

1. Dan Sullivan (2014-01-14). "Cost of the Cloud: A Developer's Guide to Reducing Your AWS Bill". PragTech Publishing. Retrieved 2014-11-27.
2. "Cloud Computing: Clash of the clouds". The Economist. 2009-10-15. Retrieved 2009-11-03
3. Semple, Bryan. (2011-07-14) "Five Capacity Management Challenges for Private Clouds," Cloud Computing Journal.
4. Cloud Computing Grows Up: Benefits Exceed Expectations According to Report. Press Release, May 21, 2013.

15

Integrating ICT in Education: Examining Needs, Barriers and Recommendations

Introduction

Information Communication Technologies are the power that has changed many aspects of the lives. The education is a socially oriented activity. It plays vital role in building the society. The quality education traditionally is associated with strong teachers having high degrees. Using ICTs in education it moved to more student –centered learning As world is moving rapidly towards digital information, the role of ICTs in education becoming more and more important and this importance will continue to grow and develop in 21st century. This paper highlights various impacts of ICT on contemporary education and also discusses the major barriers faced in the process of integration. The paper argues the role of ICT in transforming teacher-centered learning to competency based learning. It also explores some recommendations to overcome those barriers.

Information and Communication Technologies (ICT) that are becoming increasingly pervasive in societies around the world are also reaching schools. With numerous global advancements in ICT it is essential that educators have a thorough working knowledge of these media and their influence on the performance and engagement of their students. There is no firm agreement on the definition of ICT, as these technologies evolve almost daily. The 21st Century Society is an entrepreneurial Society- A century of knowledge and century of mind. Knowledge explosion, communication revolution, technology advancement, application of science to all aspects of life and above all rising aspirations of the society are the hallmarks of this century.

Use of ICT In Teaching Learning

Teaching at School, mostly, concentrates on giving information which is not the sole objective of Teaching. Along with giving information, the other objectives are:

1. developing understanding and application of the concepts
2. development of reasoning power and decision making ability
3. improving comprehension, speed and vocabulary
4. developing self-concept and study habits
5. developing proper study habits
6. developing tolerance, risk taking capacity, scientific temper, etc.

In India with the present infrastructure, class size, availability of teachers, quality of teachers, training of teachers, etc., it is difficult to realize all the objectives. As the objectives are multi-dimensional in nature, multiple methods should be used in an integrated fashion in teaching learning. At present ICT may be of some use. It is a well known fact that not a single teacher is capable of giving up to date and complete information in his own subject. The ICT can fill this gap because it can provide access to different sources of information.

Use of ICT in Diagnostic Testing & Remedial Teaching

Computer Based Diagnostic Tests will help the teachers as well as students in identifying the gray area of each and every student. This can be put on the website of the school and the student can access to it from home also. The student can learn the topic and can take the test to find exactly what he has not understood. The teacher cannot do this manually. The student progress can be monitored and his performance can be improved. This will develop confidence in students and may change their attitude towards the subject. It may also help in reducing the suicidal tendency among students. Students may start enjoying learning. The Remedial Teaching can be done by the teacher if some common mistakes are identified. It may not be feasible to organize remedial programme for individual students.

Use of ICT in Evaluation

At present the paper pencil tests are conducted for evaluating the academic performance of students. The content coverage is poor and students cannot use them on their own. These tests are evaluated by the teachers and they may not give feedback immediately to each and every student. It may be due to this that students are unable to know their weakness and do not make any attempt to improve upon them. The ICT can be made use in the evaluation. The test can be used by individual student to evaluate his learning. The student can instantaneously get the feedback about the status of his understanding. It goes a long way in improving the learning and teacher has no role to play in it. Such tests can be uploaded on the website for wider use. The students from other institutes can also make use of it. Not only the students even the teachers can also use it to assess their own understanding of the subject.

Use of ICT in Psychological Testing

The psychological testing is laborious and involves money and time. This is the age of digital technology. It can be used to digitalize all the psychological tests including the scoring and evaluation. The same may be available on the website and students and teachers can use them whenever required. Even student can use it individually and can share the result with the teacher who can help the student to improve his academic performance. The digitalized psychological tests will be easy to use and economical also.

Use of ICT in Developing Virtual Laboratory

If the Virtual Laboratory is developed, it can provide lots of freedom to students. The students can manipulate any attribute or variable related to the experiment and can see how it affects the outcome. The Virtual Laboratory can be developed using ICT. It may be made available at the door step of each and every student by uploading it on the Website.

Use of ICT in Online Tutoring

Online tutoring makes the students stay at their home. They logs in to their tutor through the use of Internet and software. It will make the academic life of many students easy. This is also how the knowledge power available in India can be made use of other countries.

Use of ICT in Developing Instructional Material

There are many teachers who are well known for their specialties in the subject. Their lectures should be digitalized and made available to all the users. It will enhance the quality of instruction in the classrooms. The teacher can use them in the classrooms and can organize discussion after it wherein the new points can be added both by the teacher as well as students. It will make the teaching effective, participatory and enjoyable.

Barriers of Integration of ICT in Education

Teacher Level Barriers

1. Several researchers indicate that one barrier that prevents teachers from using ICT in their teaching is lack of confidence. Beggs (2000) asserted the teachers "fear of failure" caused a lack of confidence.
2. The second teacher level barrier is the lack of knowledge and skills to use computers in their teaching process.
3. Resistance to change and negative attitudes towards ICT is one of the important teacher related barriers.

School Level Barriers

1. Lack of time for teachers in many aspects of their work as it affects their ability to complete tasks, with some of the teachers specifically stating which aspects of ICT require more time.

2. There are not enough training opportunities for teachers in the use of ICT's in a classroom environment. Lack of opportunities for professional development obstructed them from integrating technology in certain subjects such as science and maths.
3. Lack of access to resources in schools discourages teachers from integrating new technologies into education.
4. Lack of Technical support was found to be a major barrier for teachers in the integration of ICT in education.

Government Commitment to the Use of ICT in Schools in India

India has one of the lowest "pupils to computers ratio" in the world. Much investment is required for the provision of dedicated ICT rooms where pupils would gain 'hands on' experience of using Excel, Word, PowerPoint, Video conference, Internet etc. The poor investment by the government to the schools in integrating the ICT is seen in India.

Barriers in the Process of Preparing the Teachers

In the majority of teacher education programme offered in India, the syllabi exhibit less weight to practical than theoretical aspects. Since the nature of ICT subjects is more practical and application-oriented, there needs to be more practical than theoretical input in our curriculum related to teacher education.

Recommendations in the Integrating the ICT in Education

Recognizing the importance of ICT in education, ICT has been included as a core course at the B.Ed level in the colleges. Teacher Trainees need more structured support of ICT development from their educational institutions. There must be congruence between the school curriculum and teacher training curriculum. Otherwise, teachers are not ready to utilize their knowledge to effectively design teaching/learning processes, project work, and assignments. In addition to offering ICT as a compulsory and special course, integrated approaches need to be studied along with methods courses. This will help pupil-teachers to develop the concept of 'techno pedagogy' to a greater extent.

Enrolling the teachers for online professionally development courses. There are many websites offering free training modules. Enrolling for the best commercially available ICT training programs. The teachers should attend the ICT related courses, seminars, conferences and workshop for their professional development. The schools which are committed to preparing students for the future information society empower them to become more active learners constructing their own learning situations. In this learning mode, ICT applications become vital and more user-oriented. In this case the physical environment is made more suitable for learning individually and in small groups. Government cooperation is necessary for implementing the ICT programmes to have substantial impact and be sustainable. The active participation of the Government is essential to ensure the sector-wise introduction of ICT. Prioritizing and Planning Access to Remote Areas and Special consideration should be given to ICT connectivity and accessibility for educational purposes.

Conclusion

The role of ICTs in the education is recurring and unavoidable. Rapid changes in the technologies are indicating that the role of ICT in future will grow tremendously in education. ICT also focuses modification of the role of teachers. In addition to classroom teaching, they will have other skills and responsibilities. Teachers will act as virtual guides for students who use electronic media. Ultimately, the use of ICT will enhance the learning experiences of students. Also it helps them to think independently and communicate creatively. It also helps students for building successful careers and lives, in an increasingly technological world.

16

Models of Blended Learning Programs

Introduction

This Article highlights the Models of Blended learning programs. The majority of blended-learning programs resemble one of four models: Rotation, Flex, A La Carte, and Enriched Virtual. The Rotation model includes four sub-models: Station Rotation, Lab Rotation, Flipped Classroom, and Individual Rotation.

Blended learning is a formal education program in which a student learns at least in part through online delivery of content and instruction with some element of student control over time, place, path or pace. It is the face-to-face classroom methods that are combined with computer-mediated activities. Blended learning occurs within a face-to-face class that happens at a specific place and time. Blended learning combines the support of classroom learning with the flexibility of e-learning. Blended learning is a term increasingly used to describe the way e-learning being combined with traditional classroom methods and independent study to create a new, hybrid teaching methodology. It represents a much greater change in basic technique than simply adding computers to classrooms; it represents, in many cases, a fundamental change in the way teachers and students approach the learning experience.

Models of Blended Learning Programs

The majority of blended-learning programs resemble one of four models. They are

1. Rotation
2. Flex
3. A La Carte
4. Enriched virtual

1. Rotation model

A program in which within a given course or subject (e.g., math), students rotate between learning modalities, at least one of which is online learning. Other modalities might include activities such as small-group or full-class instruction, group projects, individual tutoring, and pencil-and-paper assignments.

a. Station Rotation (also referred to as Classroom Rotation or In-Class Rotation) — A Rotation-model implementation in which within a given course or subject (e.g., math), students rotate on a fixed schedule or at the teacher's discretion among classroom-based learning modalities. The rotation includes at least one station for online learning. Other stations might include activities such as small-group or full-class instruction, group projects, individual tutoring, and pencil-and-paper assignments. Some implementations involve the entire class alternating among activities together, whereas others divide the class into small-group or one-by-one rotations. The Station Rotation model differs from the Individual Rotation model because students rotate through all of the stations, not only those on their custom schedules.

b. Lab Rotation — A Rotation-model implementation in which within a given course or subject (e.g., math), students rotate on a fixed schedule or at the teacher's discretion among locations on the brick-and-mortar campus. At least one is a learning lab for predominantly online learning, and the other(s) are classroom(s) for other learning modalities. The Lab Rotation model differs from the Station Rotation model because students rotate among locations on the campus instead of staying in one classroom for the blended course or subject.

c. Flipped Classroom — A Rotation-model implementation in which within a given course or subject (e.g.. math), students rotate on a fixed schedule between face-to-face teacher-guided practice (or projects) on campus during the standard school day and online delivery of content and instruction of the same subject from a remote location (often home) after school. The primary delivery of content and instruction is online, which differentiates a Flipped Classroom from students who are merely doing homework practice online at night. The Flipped Classroom model accords with the idea that blended learning includes some element of student control over time, place, path, and/or pace because the model allows students to choose the location where they receive content and instruction online.

d. Individual Rotation — A Rotation-model implementation in which within a given course or subject (e.g., math), students rotate on an individually customized, fixed schedule among learning modalities, at least one of which is online learning. An algorithm or teacher sets individual student schedules. The Individual Rotation model differs from the other Rotation models because students do not necessarily rotate to each available station or modality.

2. Flex model

A program in which the online learning is the backbone of student learning, even if it directs students to offline activities at times. Students move on an individually customized, fluid schedule among learning modalities, and the teacher of record is on-site. The teacher-of-record or other adults provide face-to-face support on a flexible and adaptive as-needed basis through activities such as small-group instruction, group projects, and individual tutoring. Some implementations have substantial face-to-face support, and others have minimal (e.g., some Flex models may have face-to-face certified teachers who supplement the online learning on a daily basis, whereas others may provide little face-to-face enrichment; others may have different staffing combinations; these are useful modifiers to describe a particular Flex model).

3. A La Carte model (formerly Self-Blend model)

A program in which students take one or more courses entirely online with an online teacher of record and at the same time continue to have brick-and-mortar educational experiences. Students may take the online courses either on the brick-and-mortar campus or off-site. This differs from full-time online learning and the Enriched Virtual model because it is not a whole-school experience.

4. Enriched Virtual model

A whole-school experience in which within each course (e.g., math), students divide their time between attending a brick-and-mortar campus and learning remotely using online delivery of content and instruction. Many Enriched Virtual programs began as full-time online schools and then developed blended programs to provide students with brick-and-mortar school experiences. The Enriched Virtual model differs from the Flipped Classroom because in Enriched Virtual programs, students seldom attend the brick-and-mortar campus every weekday. It differs from the A La Carte model because it is a whole-school experience, not a course-by-course model.

Conclusion

Blended learning use as the tools of the provincial learning management system to teach and support learning in a face-to-face class. Through blended learning, students can access high-quality course materials, course calendars, and assignments during and outside school hours. Students can also take part in face-to-face lessons and communicate with their teacher and classmates using a suite of secure online tools inside the password-protected learning management system.

References

1. Bonk,C.J., & Graham, C.R. (2006). The handbook of blended learning environments: Global perspectives, local designs. San Francisco: Jossey Bass/Pfeiffer. p.5.

2. Garrison, D. R., & Kanuka, H. (2004). Blended learning: Uncovering its transformative potential in higher education. The Internet and Higher Education, 7, 95–105.

3. Harel Caperton, Idit. (2012) Learning to Make Games for Impact. The Journal of Media Literacy, 59(1), 28-38.

4. Staker and Horn (2012) "Blended Learning " (PDF). Retrieved 2013-10-24.

17

Educational-Digital skill

Introduction

There is a tremendous revolution in science and technology. Information in communication technologies have a deep cultural revolution changing. There is a need to make a realistic assessment of what technology cannot do to reach a plateau of productivity when the technology consistently delivers to realistic goals.

The impact of science and technology among students:

Digital skill is a vast technique used by all people. Educational technology and mobile learning, multi- media learning are all digital skill. Science is a boon. Man has discovered many wonderful things from the treasure of developing every day. It has made our life easier, happier and more secure. Science and technology has conquered time and space. It has made very good communication and made the transport easier. With the help of science and technology, modern medicine and medical treatments, the doctors save the life of sick people from the jaws of death. Many organs are now transplanted. It is used in the field of agriculture. The impact of science and technology among students in the field is both good and bad.

Science laboratory, space centre ISRO are taken in the highest form. Television, telecommunication, type- recorder, films, LCD projectors, digital and white board, e- learning, e-teaching, teleconferencing, teaching machine cell phones such as all types of multimedia are boons to us. But the students are affected by this because of misusing. So they blamed science. We cannot blame science. It is a wonderful boon.

Digital skill in website

By the wrong use of face book, web site, web-camera, especially cell phones, net connection, lab top etc. Science and technology become down. But once for all where we use science and technology in proper, correct and perfect way it is a boon to us otherwise it is curse and demon to us.

A secondary Information and Communication Technology curriculum should contribute to the building up of teams of professionals with these new competencies. The use of Information and Communication Technology cuts across all aspects of economic and social life. Technological developments in Information and Communication Technology are very rapid. Technology quickly becomes obsolete requiring new skills and knowledge to be mastered frequently. Adaptation is only possible when based on a sound understanding of the principles and concepts of Information and Communication Technology.

Review of Literature

Lei, Jing (2010) studied on Quantity versus Quality: A New Approach to Examine the Relationship between Technology Use and Student Outcomes. It is found that that to examine the relationship between technology use and student outcomes, the quality of technology use—how, and what, technology is used—is a more significant factor than the quantity of technology use—how much technology is used. This argument was exemplified by an empirical study that used both angles to examine the association between technology use and student outcomes. When only the quantity of technology use was examined, no significant association was observed. However, when the quality of technology was examined by investigating the specific types of technology uses, a significant association was identified between technology use and all student outcomes. Furthermore, different types of technology use showed different influences on specific student outcomes. General technology uses were positively associated with student technology proficiency, while subject-specific technology uses were negatively associated with student technology proficiency. Social-communication technology uses were significantly positively associated with developmental outcomes such as self-esteem and positive attitude towards school. Entertainment/exploration technology use showed significant positive association with student learning habits. None of these technology uses had significant influence on student academic outcome.

Chen, Rong-Ji (2010) studied on Investigating Models for Preservice Teachers' Use of Technology to Support Student-Centered Learning. The study addressed two limitations of previous research on factors related to teachers' integration of technology in their teaching. It attempted to test a structural equation model (SEM) of the relationships among a set of variables influencing preservice teachers' use of technology specifically to support student-centered learning. A review of literature led to a path model that provided the design and analysis for the study, which involved 206 preservice teachers in the United States. The results show that the proposed model had a moderate fit to the observed data, and a more parsimonious model was found to have a better fit. In addition, preservice teachers' self-efficacy of teaching with technology had the strongest influence on technology use, which was mediated by their perceived value of teaching and learning with technology. School's contextual factors had moderate influence on technology use. Moreover, the effect of preservice teachers' training on student-centered technology use was mediated by both perceived value and self-efficacy of technology. The implications for teacher preparation include close collaboration between teacher education program and field experience, focusing on specific technology uses.

Eisenberg, Mike; Johnson, Doug; Berkowitz, Bob (2010) studied on Information, Communications, and Technology (ICT) Skills

Curriculum Based on the Big6 Skills Approach to Information Problem-Solving. There is clear and widespread agreement among the public and educators that all students need to be proficient technology users. Technology literacy is among the attributes that appear in nearly every set of "21st Century Skills." However, while districts spend a great deal of money on technology, there seems to be only a vague notion of what technology literacy really means. Defining and describing technology skills is only a first step to assure all children become proficient information and technology users. Other critical elements will include a teacher-supported scope and sequence of skills, well designed projects, and effective assessments. Equally essential is fruitful collaboration among classroom teachers, teacher librarians, and technology teachers in order to present students with a unified and integrated approach to ensure that all children master the skills they will need to thrive in an information-rich future. This article presents the "Information, Communications, and Technology (ICT) Skills for Information Problem Solving" curriculum which defines technology capabilities and identifies associated skills based on the Big6 Skills Approach. The Curriculum describes levels of technology proficiency, and in so doing, promotes the skills and concepts basic to information and technology. In an information society, it is essential that students are technologically productive and able to solve information problems effectively and efficiently. This curriculum requires more than teaching computer skills, technology hardware, and software programs in an isolated approach. An effective technology curriculum must be integrated across content areas and grade levels to improve the learning process. Technology is successfully integrated when it seamlessly supports curricular goals. Students learn and refine their technology skills when they work on projects that require them to solve problems and make decisions.

Savage, Robert S.; Erten, Ozlem; Abrami, Philip; Hipps, Geoffrey; Comaskey, Erin; van Lierop, Dea (2010) studied on ABRACADABRA in the Hands of Teachers: The Effectiveness of a Web-Based Literacy Intervention in Grade 1 Language Arts Programs. Each teacher chose to use the program in qualitatively distinct ways that corresponded to the first three stages of Sandholtz, Ringstaff, and Dwyer's (1997) technology integration model, namely: "Entry," "Adoption" and "Adaptation." Growth in literacy between pre- and post-test revealed significant differences associated with technology integration style across all measures of literacy and related language skills. The largest and most-widespread effects were evident for the "Adaptation" group that linked technology content to wider learning themes in the classroom. In terms of overall growth in standardised literacy scores across all six such measures used, Adaptation proved to be 60% more effective than Adoption. Results suggest that explorations of exactly how teachers use technology have important implications for practice as well as for the interpretation of field-based studies of the effectiveness of educational technology.

Jun, Han; Zhuzhu, Wang (2010) studied on Capability Building in Educational Technology for Teachers in China. This paper gives a brief introduction to the project called Education Technology Capacity Building Plan for All Primary and Secondary Teachers now being implemented in China. Because information and communication technology skills training cannot match the demand of teachers' professional development, the Chinese Ministry of Education established the education technology standard for teachers and launched the project. This paper introduced the features of standard training and testing, and discusses the output and influence of the project.

McGarr, Oliver (2010) studied on Education for Sustainable Development in Technology Education in Irish Schools: A Curriculum Analysis. This paper explores the integration of Education for Sustainable Development (ESD) in technology education and the extent to which it is currently addressed in curriculum documents and state examinations in technology education at post-primary level in Ireland. This analysis is conducted amidst the backdrop of considerable change in technology education at post-primary level. The analysis of the provision of technology education found, that among the range of technology related subjects offered, the study of Technology and Society is only addressed in one in a comprehensive manner. The paper discusses the implications of this limited integration, examines the factors inhibiting greater integration of ESD and outlines opportunities for future development.

Waring, Scott M. (2010) studied on The Impact of a Technology Coordinator's Belief System upon Using Technology to Create a Community's History. As it has been shown that teachers of social studies content are less likely than teachers of other content areas to utilize technology in their classroom, this study focuses on one instructional technology coordinators' beliefs towards technology, instruction, and students and how these beliefs impacted how technology was utilized during a technology-enriched community history project with a group of fourth-grade students. It was determined that the instructional technology coordinators' beliefs included the following: (a) technology should serve as a tool and should be seamlessly integrated into the curriculum; (b) the teacher should construct meaningful experiences that allow students to become engaged in the learning process; however, before guiding student discovery, the teacher needs to explicitly teach basic technological skills; (c) and all students are able to learn and are capable of engaging in independent problem solving and critical thinking at some level. Her beliefs manifested themselves daily, particularly in the way that she approached instruction and integrated technology seamlessly into the curriculum. Through this study, it was found that the technology coordinator's beliefs toward technology, instruction, and her students directly impacted how technology was used in her classroom.

Jun, Han; Zhuzhu, Wang (2010) studied on Capability Building in Educational Technology for Teachers in China. This paper gives a brief introduction to the project called Education Technology Capacity Building Plan for All Primary and Secondary Teachers now being implemented in China. Because information and communication technology skills training cannot match the demand of teachers' professional development, the Chinese Ministry of Education established the education technology standard for teachers and launched the project. This paper introduced the features of standard training and testing, and discusses the output and influence of the project.

Ruzic-Dimitrijevic, Ljiljana; Dimitrijevic, Maja (2010) studied on Challenges IT Instructors Face in the Self-Education Process. We find that the earlier the instructors graduated, the smaller is the chance they studied the technologies similar to the ones they teach. We found that none of the surveyed instructors who graduated before 1979 teach a technology they studied. The analysis of the survey also supports the second hypothesis. The results show that 70% of the IT instructors have to change the course syllabus every 2-3 years due to the technology changes. We also found that the majority of the instructors primarily use textbooks and online tutorials to self teach new technologies, which supports the third hypothesis. By comparison, they take courses given by others and work on real life projects far less often. In contrast, most instructors agree that taking courses and working on projects would greatly help them in their self-education. Most instructors (16 out of 20) assert that the lack of time stops them from doing so, which according to the survey is found to be one of the major challenges they face in the process of self-education, supporting the fourth hypothesis. Considering the results of our research, as well as our own experience, we have identified a list of activities that make the process of self-education more efficient and/or effective for IT instructors. These activities include taking on-line tutorials, creating software programs using the environment/ language/tools covered in the courses, working on real life projects, taking organized courses, attending IT/CS conferences, seminars, and workshops, collecting experience from industry people, and using the help of advanced students. However, in order to create the time for IT instructors to apply the self-learning methods and stay on top of the new technologies, we conclude that it may be necessary that the university policy include the time for self-learning as a significant part of IT instructors' everyday duties, i.e., as a part of their "job description".

Larson, Lotta; Kuhn, Cyndi Danner; Collins, Royce Ann; Balthazor, Gerri; Ribble, Mike; Miller, Teresa Northern (2009) studied on Technology Instruction: Fixing the Disconnect. High school students spend much of their educational journeys immersed in "old" literacies of paper, pencil, and print books. But outside of the classroom, they are exposed to information and communication technologies—such as blogs, wikis, Internet browsers, multimedia, social networking sites, and a wide range of software—each of which demand new literacies. This disconnect is a serious problem for schools because it reflects a decline in school's relevancy to students' futures, and the gap between how schools teach and how students learn will only grow over time. The first step in updating a school's technology and instruction is to revisit and revise current vision statements by facilitating conversations with all stakeholders about expectations for student skills upon graduation. Vision setting must include the new literacies. Teachers and education leaders must model expectations and support visionary teaching and learning through technology. To make that happen, they need instructional technology specialists who not only have a strong knowledge of hardware, networks, and equipment maintenance but also understand the art of teaching and how to enhance and enrich the daily curriculum by integrating technology. To do this, instructional technology staff members and those creating the curriculum must engage in ongoing dialogue to ensure that computer language is translated into the language of teaching and is directly related to what teachers want to do in their classrooms. For schools to successfully integrate technology, leaders must encourage and support strong relationships between teachers and technology support staff members. Schools must also provide easy access to technology in classrooms so that teachers can effectively integrate technology into the curriculum. Limited resources and complicated check-out procedures often contribute to lack of use. In addition, frustrations over blocked sites or limited access to online resources prevent teachers from integrating technology. Leaders, teachers, and technology staff members need ongoing communication with one another to share needs, frustrations, and solutions. Schools must move ahead quickly. It may be understandable for teachers and leaders to be a bit behind in the use of technology, but it is no longer adequate or appropriate to hold students back. Students today will be leaders in a global society, and technology can connect them to that world in ways that were unimaginable 10 years ago. School leaders need to join students in their world—which includes all of the new literacies—so that everyone can function and contribute to the future.

Objectives

1. To study the level of teachers attitude towards using new technology in teaching
2. To find out whether there is any significant relationship between teachers attitude towards the use of new technology and their interest in teaching.

Methodology

The methodology adopted for the study is explained in detail. The sampling technique, size of the sample, variables of the study, description of the tool used and administration of tool are elaborated.

Sample

The study was conducted on 100 school teachers, Coimbatore district, Tamil Nadu.

Data Collection

Primary data, required for the present research work were collected by conducting direct interviews using questionnaire. All the respondents were given sufficient information about the study. These respondents were provided with the same questionnaires. They were also informed that they have to answer in the same fashion.

Analysis and Interpretation

Gender and attitude towards the use of new technology

Null Hypothesis No. 1

There is no significant difference between male and female teachers attitude towards the use of new technology.

Table 1

The Significance of the difference ('t' value) between mean scores of male and female teacher's attitude towards the use of new technology

Gender	N	Mean	SD	't' value	Level of Significance (0.05)
Male	50	100.30	11.81	4.89	Significant
Female	50	107.30	12.57		

It is evident from the table the calculated 't' value is 4.89 is significant at 0.05 level. Hence, the framed null hypothesis is rejected and research hypothesis is accepted. It is inferred that there is significant difference found between male and female teachers attitude towards the use of new technology.

Qualification and attitude towards the use of new technology Null Hypothesis No. 2

There is no significant difference between undergraduate and post graduate teachers with respect to their attitude towards the use of new technology.

Table 2

The significance of the difference ('t' value) between undergraduate and post graduate teachers with respect to their attitude towards the use of new technology.

Qualification	N	Mean	SD	't' value	Level of Significance (0.05)
Under graduate	35	103.64	11.44	0.28	Not Significant
Post graduate	65	103.23	13.53		

It is evident from the table the calculated 't' value is 0.28 which is not significant at 0.05 level. Hence, the framed null hypothesis is accepted. It shows that there is no significant difference between undergraduate and post graduate teachers with respect to their attitude towards the use of new technology.

Locality of the School and attitude towards the use of new technology Null Hypothesis No. 3

There is no significant difference between rural and urban school teachers attitude towards the use of new technology.

It is evident from the table the calculated 't' value is 0.06 which is not significant at 0.05 level. Hence, the framed null hypothesis is accepted. It shows that there is no significant difference between rural and urban school teachers attitude towards the use of new technology.

Table 3

The Significance of the difference ('t' value) between rural and urban school teachers attitude towards the use of new technology

Locality of the school	N	Mean	SD	't' value	Level of Significance (0.05)
Rural	65	103.42	11.23	0.06	Not Significant
Urban	35	103.33	14.15		

Type of School and attitude towards the use of new technology

Null Hypothesis No. 4

There is no significant difference between private and government school teachers attitude towards the use of new technology.

Table 4

The Significance of the difference ('t' value) between private and government school teachers attitude towards the use of new technology

Type of School	N	Mean	SD	't' value	Level of Significance (0.05)
Private	65	104.79	11.54	1.26	Not Significant
Government	35	102.78	13.01		

It is evident from the table the calculated 't' value is 1.26 which is not significant at 0.05 level. Hence, the framed null hypothesis is accepted. It shows that there is no significant difference between private and government school teachers attitude towards the use of new technology.

Level of teaching and attitude towards the use of new technology

Null Hypothesis No. 5

There is no significant difference between secondary and higher secondary school teachers attitude towards the use of new technology.

It is evident from the table the calculated 't' value is 1.85 which is not significant at 0.05 level. Hence, the framed null hypothesis is accepted. It is inferred that there is no significant difference between secondary and higher secondary school teachers attitude towards the use of new technology.

Table 5

The Significance of the difference ('t' test) between secondary and higher secondary school teachers attitude towards the use of new technology

Level of teaching	N	Mean	SD	't' value	Level of Significance (0.05)
Secondary School	60	102.12	12.12	1.85	Not Significant
Higher secondary School	40	104.82	13.03		

Teaching Experience and attitude towards the use of new technology Null Hypothesis No. 6

There is no significant difference among teachers who have different years of teaching experience with respect to their attitude towards the use of new technology.

Table 6

The Significance of the difference ('F' test) among school teachers with respect to their attitude towards the use of new technology

Teaching Experience	Sum of Squares	Mean Squares	df	'F' Value	Level of Significance (0.05)
Between Groups	2281.690	1140.845	2	7.48	Significant
Within Groups	45273.227	152.435	97		
Total	47554.917	-	99		

It is evident from the table the calculated 'F' value is 7.48 which is significant at 0.05 level. Hence, the framed null hypothesis is rejected and research hypothesis is accepted. It is inferred that there is significant difference among teachers who have different years of teaching experience with respect to their attitude towards the use of new technology.

From table, it is revealed that there is significant difference between teachers who have below 10 years of teaching experience and 10-20 years of teaching experience and teachers who have above

20 years of teaching experience and below 10 years of teaching experience. Whereas no significant difference is found between teachers who have above 20 years of teaching experience and 10-20 years of teaching experience.

Table 7

The Significance of the difference ('t' test) between teachers who have different years of teaching experience with respect to their attitude towards the use of new technology

Teaching experience	N	Mean	SD	't' value	Level of Significance (0.05)
Below 10 years	49	109.33	11.05	3.06	Significant
10-20 years	20	103.03	12.80		
Above 20 years	31	101.67	12.47	4.16	Significant
Below 10 years	49	109.33	11.05		
10-20 years	20	103.03	12.80	0.81	Not Significant
Above 20 years	31	101.67	12.47		

Correlation Analysis

Correlation Analysis between teachers attitude towards the use of new technology and interest in teaching

One of the important objectives of the present investigation is to study the significant relationship between teacher's attitude towards the use of new technology and interest in teaching. For this purpose, the investigator applied the co-efficient of correlation ('r'). The computed values are given in the table. The investigator also framed a null hypothesis for testing the relationship between teacher's attitude towards the use of new technology and interest in teaching.

Null hypothesis No. 8

There is no significant relationship between teacher's attitude towards the use of new technology and interest in teaching.

It is evident from the table the computed correlation coefficient 'r' for entire sample is 0.56, which is significant at 0.05 level. Hence, the framed null hypothesis is rejected. It is inferred that there is significant relationship found between teacher's attitude towards the use of new technology and their interest in teaching.

Table 8

Co-efficient of Correlation between teacher's attitude towards the use of new technology and interest in teaching

Correlation	N	'r' value	Level of Significance at 0.05 level
Teacher's attitude towards the use of new technology and interest in teaching	100	0.56	Significant

Suggestions

The present study gives a clear-cut view about the present position of teachers attitude towards the use of new technology and their interest in teaching. Based on the important findings stated earlier the following recommendations are suggested.

1. Teachers must be provided with adequate opportunities to enhance their knowledge in new technologies and equipments. The government should provide more effective environment through schools for them to improve their skills in application of new technologies in teaching.
2. Periodical in-service training programmes should be organized to keep their interest and quest in teaching.
3. The finding of the present study reveals that the teachers have neutral attitude towards the use of new technology in teaching and low interest in teaching. This indicates that the Heads of the institutions must look into the varied problems that influence the interest of teachers and find amicable solutions to their difficulties.
4. More activities should be planned in the curriculum to bring forth different modes of creative expressions which will provide competition and generate interest of teachers in teaching.
5. Sincere work and involved performances of teachers must be recognized and honoured by the authorities. And application

of innovative methods and technologies in instruction must be encouraged.

6. In addition with the above recommendation the government and all the other concerned authorities should realize the problems of experienced teachers and provide conductive environment of growth and mutual help of teachers should be ensured.

Conclusion

The present study is conducted on teachers attitude towards the use of new technologies in teaching and their interest in teaching. The findings of the present study revealed that the teachers have neutral attitude towards the use of new technology and low interest in teaching. Therefore, the authorities and government should find suitable measures to improve the interest of teachers in teaching and the application of innovative technologies in Teaching Learning Process.

References

1. Larson, Lotta; Kuhn, Cyndi Danner; Collins, Royce Ann; Balthazor, Gerri; Ribble, Mike; Miller, Teresa Northern (2009) Technology Instruction: Fixing the Disconnect. Principal Leadership, v10 n4 p54-58.
2. Chen, Rong-Ji (2010) Investigating Models for Preservice Teachers' Use of Technology to Support Student-Centered Learning. Computers & Education, v55 n1 p32-42.
3. Eisenberg, Mike; Johnson, Doug; Berkowitz, Bob (2010) Information, Communications, and Technology (ICT) Skills Curriculum Based on the Big6 Skills Approach to Information Problem-Solving. Library Media Connection, v28 n6 p24-27.
4. Jun, Han; Zhuzhu, Wang(2010) Capability Building in Educational Technology for Teachers in China British Journal of Educational Technology, v41 n4 p607-611.
5. Lei, Jing (2010) Quantity versus Quality: A New Approach to Examine the Relationship between Technology Use and Student Outcomes. 2010.

6. Lesisko, Lee J.; Wright, Robert J.; O'Hern, Brenda (2010) Technology Integration: A Best Practice Perspective. Online Submission, Paper presented at the Annual Meeting of the Eastern Educational Research Association (Savannah, GA, Feb 10-13, 2010).
7. McGarr, Oliver (2010) Education for Sustainable Development in Technology Education in Irish Schools: A Curriculum Analysis. International Journal of Technology and Design Education, v20 n3 p317-332.
8. Ruzic-Dimitrijevic, Ljiljana; Dimitrijevic, Maja (2010) Challenges IT Instructors Face in the Self-Education Process. Journal of Information Technology Education, v9 pIIP-35-IIP-48.
9. Savage, Robert S.; Erten, Ozlem; Abrami, Philip; Hipps, Geoffrey; Comaskey, Erin; van Lierop, Dea (2010) ABRACADABRA in the Hands of Teachers: The Effectiveness of a Web-Based Literacy Intervention in Grade 1 Language Arts Programs . Computers & Education, v55 n2 p911-922.
10. Shapley, Kelly; Sheehan, Daniel; Maloney, Catherine; Caranikas-Walker, Fanny (2010) Effects of Technology Immersion on Teachers' Growth in Technology Competency, Ideology, and Practices. Journal of Educational Computing Research, v42 n1 p1-33.

18

Empowering A Digital Learning Environment For Teaching Grammar

Introduction

Grammar is the modus operandi that administrates the practice of English language. A strong foundation and establishment of English grammar is therefore of the greatest importance. Most non-native English speakers commit grammatical errors while conversing in English. Improving grammar consumes time and effort but it is well worth it. When Grammar is imparted through digital technology, they prepare students in a better manner to be vital thinkers of online content; personalize learning for students and teachers; enable students to regulate their own learning better; offer students with more high quality feedback from both teachers and other students; and sustain a successful implementation of the Common Core Standards. Students as critical thinkers of online content will:

- Identify and classify a problem
- Trace information
- Appraise information

- Amalgamate information
- Correspond information

The quantum of information accessible online is overwhelming. An essential accomplishment feature in life is being proficient to locate information on-line, assess the trustworthiness of the resource, blend information from manifold resources, and correspond the findings. Common Core standards require to educate students these significant skills used for conducting on-line research and solving problems in math, English Language arts, science and social studies, and the technical areas . Technology sanctions primary shifts in the plan of classroom learning environments. Each of the design elements below describes a transformative change in how classrooms can be reorganized by leveraging technology, often by scaling up teachers' abilities to provide feedback and personalize instruction. Students as self reflective regulators of their learning gain access to learning content and skills dynamically through a device they control as opposed to accessing information from one human being, a rotating set of classroom books, or limited access to media center labs. When devices are used in a group setting, students can work more actively and collaboratively as they access information, solve problems, and communicate their answers using a digital toolkit providing expanded means of self-expression.But the question here is how far they can excel in dealing with grammar. Below given are some valid criteria to be contemplated :

Comprehending the edifice of grammar

The pivotal concern is to discern the different building blocks of grammar like noun pronoun, adjective, adverb, article, verbs, preposition interjection and conjunction . The internet is chock-a-block of wherewithal about these and it is generally a good idea to understand them well.

Focus upon sentence structures

Paying attention to how sentences are constructed is what is most important. This practice helps ingrain different sentence structures and will help spoken and written English.

Constant Practice

As an English learner, it is extremely important to talk in English at any given opportunity. If you do not have partners to practise with, then try to speak in front of the mirror.

Handy Grammar exercises

Solving different grammar exercises will reveal the weaknesses. These exercises are freely available on the internet. It is only after the correct assessment of the weaknesses they could be rectifed.

Mentor Hunting

Many learners have improved their grammar working with a mentor. A mentor could even be a friend who has a strong command over English grammar. Real time feedback is very beneficial in improving grammar.

Using Digital Platform for Teaching Grammar

The Websites will blend the best digital tools with a standards-based curriculum, effective instructional practices, and robust teacher training and support. They will provide schools with research-based digital resources and instructional content from which teachers can choose to best address students' unique needs. Through adaptive technology platforms, students' needs are quickly diagnosed and personalized learning plans are created. These practices create immediate feedback, enabling students to progress at their own pace, time and place of learning. Technology also empowers student voice for those who are better able to communicate with the help of technology. Examples include threaded on-line discussions (where students who may be too shy to speak up in class feel comfortable writing their thoughts), assistive technology and improved access to powerful graphic design and multi-media tools for students who may be more facile showing rather than speaking their ideas.

Trends Driving Digital Learning

The following are the trends which drive digital learning in a progressive mode:

1. Student centered personalized learning

2. Common Core: new expectations driving shifts in instruction that create new demands for education resources, interventions, tools.
3. Explosion of innovative learning tools and services
4. Fiscal climate is still challenging. New normal for foreseeable future requires leaders to do more with same resources.
5. Big Data from new integrated systems that can be used for personalized and adaptive learning, new accountability models, and richer analytics.

Samples of Some Websites and the Quintessence of Content Given in those Websites http://www.englishclub.com/grammar/

Welcome to English Club Grammar for English learners. Many of these grammar lessons also have quizzes to check your understanding. If you still don't understand something, feel free to ask a question at the Grammar. grammar (noun): the structure and system of a language, or of languages in general, usually considered to consist of syntax and morphology.

What is Grammar?

Grammar hot links Verbs | Passive voice | Modal verbs | Conditionals | Questions | Irregular verbs |Going to | Gerunds | Phrasal Verbs | Tenses | Nouns | (Un)Countable nouns | Adjectives | Articles | Preposition List

English Grammar Terms (long version)

English Grammar Terms (short version)

The 8 English Parts of Speech

These are the words that you use to make a sentence. There are only 8 types of word - and the most important is the Verb!

1. Verbs be, have, do, work
2. Nouns man, town, music
3. Adjectives a, the, 69, big
4. Adverbs loudly, well, often

5. Pronouns you, ours, some
6. Prepositions at, in, on, from
7. Conjunctions and, but, though
8. Interjections ah, dear, er, um

Grammatical Category Including number, case, gender, tense, aspect etc.

What Is A Sentence?

Reported Speech

Grammar Quizzes

1. Active or Passive Quiz
2. Adjective Order Quiz
3. Adverbs Quiz
4. Can, Could Quiz
5. Compound Nouns Quiz
6. Conditionals Quiz
7. Continuous Tense Quiz
8. Determiners Quiz
9. For or Since Quiz
10. Future Time Quiz
11. Gerunds Quiz
12. Gradable and Non-Gradable Adjectives Quiz
13. Have to, Must Quiz
14. Infinitive or -ing Quiz
15. Main Verb Forms Quiz
16. Parts of Speech Quiz
17. Past Simple Quiz
18. Past Continuous Quiz

19. Phrasal Verbs Quiz
20. Present Continuous Quiz
21. Present Perfect Quiz
22. Present Perfect Continuous Quiz
23. Present Simple Quiz
24. Proper Nouns Quiz
25. Questions Quiz
26. Subjunctive Quiz
27. Tag Questions Quiz
28. Used to do Quiz
29. More Grammar Quizzes...

Easy English Question of the Day

Check your grammar knowledge with the Question of the Day at EasyEnglish.com.In this Teach English section you'll find materials and pages designed to help in your teaching. Don't forget, there are also many resources in Learn English that will be useful for teachers.

http://www.englishgrammar.org/

Welcome to EnglishGrammar.org!Here you'll learn all aspects of the English written language, enabling you to improve your writing skills in both personal and formal communications. Whether you're starting with the very basics such as understanding the meaning of verbs and nouns and correct apostrophe placement, or wanting to understand more complex topics such as conjunctions, syntax optimization and creative writing techniques, we have it all covered.

How to Get Started

We're constantly working to make this website more effective and efficient, and we're committed to helping you find the information you need, fast. To get started, navigate over to the left-hand side of the page. There you'll see a column entitled "Topics". From that list you can choose from a broad range of subject matters, including business writing, essay writing, prepositions, pronouns, spelling, writing exercises, and a whole lot more. If there's a specific topic you want to learn more about, but don't see a heading for it under "Topics"; simply navigate to the top right-hand side of the page, and enter your query in the search box. If you're after some interactive learning, then look along the navigation bar at the top of the page. Here you can opt to download printable lessons, check your grammar online, or download the updated "2014 Grammar Guide" by signing up to the newsletter on the right-hand side of this page.

Stay in Touch

We'd love you to join our community and stay in touch on a regular basis, and there are a number of ways you can do this.

Firstly, if you would like to be first to know when we post new articles, and would like to receive awesome English grammar tips straight to your inbox, then simply enter your email address at the top of the page where it says "Get Updates". Don't worry. We won't share your email address with anyone else, and we'll only use it to contact you about things relating to improving your English grammar. Secondly, you can hop over to the Face book box on the right-hand side of the page and click 'Like'. This will ensure you see our Face book updates in your news feed. We regularly post links to new content that will help better your understanding of English grammar. Last but not least, you can also follow us on Google Plus and Twitter, too. Simply follow @Grammar Updates on Twitter and add me on Google Plus to do so.

Have a Suggestion?

Is there any subject in particular that you want to learn more about? Is there an addition we could make to the site that you think would help others with their learning too? I'd love to hear your feedback on what we can do better. Drop us an email using the contact form and we'll do our best to meet your needs. We hope you enjoy the site, and we hope you have fun improving your English grammar skills. Here's to your successful learning journey!

http: / /www.englishgrammarsecrets.com/

Use these English grammar lessons for self study or to consolidate your lessons with your teacher. There is absolutely nothing to pay but please support us by buying our books and CDs in the future. We recommend that you read the grammar explanation on the first page of the lesson and then do the exercises, thinking all the time about the rules in the grammar explanation. Remember that learning grammar is only one part of learning a language. So don't be obsessed by it! Learning examples that will help you when you speak or write is the best way to learnTop of ForBottom of Form

http://www.usingenglish.com/

Free English grammar and vocabulary worksheets and printable handouts, for English language and English as a Second Language (ESL) teachers and instructors to use in the classroom or other teaching environment.

http://www.perfect-english-grammar.com/

How to learn English:

I hope you find my grammar site useful, but grammar is only one part of learning English, or any language. We also need to practise reading, writing, speaking, listening, as well as learning new vocabulary and improving our pronunciation.

Ways to improve your English:

Read about improving your English listening here.

Read about improving your English reading here.

Read about English vocabulary and collocations here.

Read about improving your writing here.

Read about improving your English speaking here.

Above all, don't panic if you can't speak or understand or write well yet!

It takes a long time to learn a language, and learning English might be particularly difficult (it depends on your first language). If you relax and don't force yourself, then it will come.

About EnglishTeacherMelanie.com

This is a blog to help intermediate to advanced English language learners (people learning English as a foreign language) improve their English skills!

Memorizing words and grammar rules is the easy part of learning English – it's the strange pronunciation and all the expressions and cultural references that are difficult to understand! That's why this website is here, to help guide you through the maze of English. Here you'll find something to help improve each language skill: speaking, listening, and reading, as well as vocabulary and grammar explanations! This is how EnglishTeacherMelanie.com can help you improve your English. On this blog you can ...

1. Listen to the English Teacher Melanie Podcast to practice listening and improve your pronunciation
2. Watch videos to improve your pronunciation & learn new vocabulary
3. Read posts about vocabulary to learn new words
4. Read posts about grammar
5. Learn some new study tips to improve your English
6. Read about Canada: fun facts you didn't know before, Canadian holidays, life in Canada!

The above mentioned websites are exquisitely rich in grammar resources which could be utilized by the teachers of English classes. There is overwhelming information which could be generated through internet and it is up to the efficiency of the Teacher to utilize it in an adept manner.

Conclusion

The world is converted into digital, and the "y" generation is leading the pack with technology that just may make some other items archaic. As pre-teens and teenagers habitually resort to digital strategy for entertainment and work, the countenance of education may change as well. There are many merits to going digital. Typing is predisposed to go more rapidly for skilled keyboard users, which many youngsters have become since they have essentially grown up with computers in the household. This makes note taking simpler. When notes and assignments are saved to a computer, there's less possibility of them getting misplaced, especially if important files are routinely backed up. Data saved on a computer can easily be manipulated into a number of different formats, potentially making it easier to study. Bodies of text can be transformed into charts or pie graphs with many word processing programs. Students can cut and paste important quotes or examples into essays and the like, saving time on homework. In terms of streamlining backpacks, digital readers and other devices eliminate heavy books and notebooks. This can be seen as a big advantage to students who have grown accustomed to carrying around heavy weight on their backs from a very young age. As many teachers turn to online resources, such as e-mailing and posting assignments on a personal Web site, students almost have to keep up with the times with some sort of tool that has Internet access.

References

1. Auguste, B., Kihn, P., & Miller, M. (2010, September). Closing the talent gap: Attracting and retaining top-third graduates to careers in teaching. (pp. 23–25). McKinsey & Company.
2. Baker, R. 2009 Pedagogies and Digital Content in the Australian School Sector, Education.au, viewed 4 May 2010, http://www.thelearningfederation.edu.au/verve/_resources/Pedagogies_Report.pdf.
3. Department of Education and Early Childhood Development, Victoria, 2009, Expanding Horizons. Digital Learning Platforms Research Series Paper No. 1, Melbourne.

   http://www.education.vic.gov.au/researchinnovation/resources/recentpubl.htm.
4. http://www.englishteachermelanie.com/grammar/
5. http://www.grammarly.com/
6. http://www.perfect-english-grammar.com/
7. http://www.englishgrammar.org/
8. http://www.englishclub.com/grammar/

19

Progress of Open and Distance Learning

Introduction

Education is not acquiring bookish knowledge but it is a lifelong process for self development and at a large scale it is the development of the country. Besides curricular instructions, the life skills need to be integrated in the education system of India. Life skills are abilities for adaptive and positive behavior that enable individuals to deal effectively with the demands and challenges that facilitate the physical, mental and emotional well-being of student. Knowledge and life skills education imparted to the students are likely to be passed on their own children, thus influencing future generations. This is possible with the system like open and distance education learning.

Open and Distance Learning

Open and Distance Learning (ODL) system is a system wherein teachers and learners need not necessarily be present either at same place or same time and is flexible in regard to modalities and timing of teaching and learning. ODL system in India consists of State Open Universities (SOUs), Institutions and Universities offering education and includes Correspondence Course Institutes (CCIs) in conventional dual mode universities. At present there are 13 State Open Universities in India, which provide education only in the distance mode.

The mission of distance learning includes greater dimensions of openness, flexibility, and access. "Open" means the removal of constraints of face to face conventional classroom method, flexibility for students who need an alternative to the conventional system and scale with equality. "Distance" means teacher and student have a space and time division or distance, and also involves e-learning, open learning, flexible learning, on-line learning, resource-based learning, and technology-mediated learning.

Distance learning is described as "a process to create and provide access to learning when the source of information and the learners are separated by time and distance, or both"

History of ODL

1840 - Modern distance learning initially relied on the development of postal services and has been practiced since Isaac Pitman taught shorthand in Great Britain via correspondence. (Moore & Kearsley, 2005, p. 235).

1858 - The University of London claims to be the first university to offer distance learning degrees, establishing its External Program. This program is now known as the University of London International Programs and includes Postgraduate, Undergraduate and Diploma degrees created by colleges such as the London School of Economics, Royal Holloway and Goldsmiths.

1892 - In the United States William Rainey Harper, first president of the University of Chicago developed the concept of extended education, whereby the research university had satellite colleges of education in the wider community, he also encouraged the concept of correspondence school courses to further promote education, an idea that was put into practice by Columbia University (Levinson, 2005, p. 69).

1911 - In Australia, the University of Queensland established its Department of Correspondence Studies. (White, 1982, p. 262).

1968 - Charles Wide-eyed of the University of Wisconsin–Madison is considered significant in promoting methods other than the postal service to deliver distance education in America. The Carnegie Foundation funded Wedemeyer's Articulated Instructional Media Project (AIM) which brought in a variety of communications technologies aimed at providing learning to an off-campus population.

1974 - Germany's Fern Universidad in Hagen followed and now there are many similar institutions around the world, often with the name Open University (in English or in the local language). All "open universities" use distance education technologies as delivery methodologies and some have grown to become "mega-universities" (Daniel, 1998, p. 15) a term coined to denote institutions with more than 100,000 students.

History of ODL in India

Open and distance learning in India started around 1960s. By the 1980s there were 34 Universities offering correspondence education through departments designed for that purpose. The first single mode Open University was established in Andhra Pradesh in 1982, followed by the Indira Gandhi National Open University (IGNOU), and subsequently in Bihar, Rajasthan, and Maharashtra, Madhya Pradesh, Gujarat, Karnataka, West Bengal, and Uttar Pradesh (established throughout the 1980s and 1990s). The establishment of these single mode distance education universities was stimulated by the government's intention to democratize education and make it lifelong. The initiative did not discourage the expansion at the same time of correspondence programs in dual mode universities.

The year 1995 witnessed the enrollment of 200,000 students in open and distance learning, accounting for 3% of total higher education enrollment. Most open and distance learning universities in India follow the model of the UK Open University.

Need for ODL

There is a need to bring changes in the existing system where the learning time, learning style, and the pace of learning, and the evaluation system is such that it does not create any pressure and stress on the learners. The focus of the education should be on life skill development rather than making the students bookworms. The learners should be made capable of using their potential and capabilities for a happy and stress free life. For this they should be provided with an open and free environment at home as well as in the schools and colleges.

Every year 5.5 million students pass out of class X of which 3.3 million go to Class X1, leaving 2.2 million out of the educational system. By 2020, about 220 million students will pass out from school, out of which, about 150 million will not enroll for college education. ODL is needed to provide second chance to those who miss the education.

Distance Education Council

Distance Education Council (DEC) is founded in 1992. DEC is responsible for the promotion, co-ordination, and the maintenance of quality and standards. A range of factors including emerging ICTs, liberalization, privatization and globalization have amplified the demand for open and distance learning.

The DEC provides technical and financial support to the Open and Distance Education Institutes in the country. The technical help includes development of technological infrastructure, institutional reform, professional development and training, student support services, computerization and networking of improvement of quality of education. The DEC's financial help includes financial assistance to State Open Universities (SOUs) and other institutions of open and distance learning like CCIs, research grant on topics of contemporary relevance, travel grants to individuals to attend international conferences and funds for organizing seminar to institutions.

Significance

The potential impact of distance learning on all education has been emphasized by the development of Internet-based technologies, particularly the World Wide Web. Significance of distance learning are balancing inequalities between age groups, geographical expansion of education access, delivering education for large audiences, offering the combination of education with work or family life. Distance learning increases access to learning and training opportunity, provides increased opportunities for updating, retraining and personal enrichment, improves cost effectiveness of educational resources, supports the quality and variety of existing educational structures, enhances and consolidates capacity.

Another advantage of distance learning is its convenience because many of the technologies are easily accessible from home. Many forms of distance learning provide students the opportunity to participate whenever they wish, on an individual basis, because of distance learning flexibility. This kind of education is quite affordable, as many forms of distance learning involve little or no cost. Distance learning is also multi-sensory. Introverted students who are too shy to ask questions in class will often "open up" when provided an opportunity to interact via e-mail or other individualized means (Franklin, Yoakam & Warren, 1996, p. 126).

Distance Learning Methods

The methods of learning used in distance learning are divided into two basic groups: synchronous and asynchronous learning. The term synchronous learning is a mode of delivery where all participants are present at the same time. It resembles traditional classroom teaching methods despite the participants being located remotely. It requires a timetable to be organized. The asynchronous learning mode of delivery is where participants access course materials on their own schedule and so is more flexible. Students are not required to be together at the same time.

Distance Learning Technologies

The various technologies used in distance learning are print, computer, audio and video. Print materials may serve as the primary source of instruction, or they may be supplemental. As a primary source, distance students use a textbook. As a supplement to instruction, text materials may take the form of worksheets or study guides that are used in conjunction with video or voice technologies.

Supplemental print materials may be disseminated via regular mail or over the Internet. In addition, fax machines are often used to transmit the print materials back and forth between the students and the teachers.

Other technologies, such as e-mail, could then be used to ask questions and send assignments back to the teacher. Audio or voice technologies offer cost-effective ways to enhance distance learning courses. The audio component of a distance learning course can be as simple as a telephone with voicemail, or it can be as complex as an audio conference with microphones, telephone bridges and speakers. Audio files and CDs are inexpensive, easily duplicated and very versatile and it is used to deliver lectures, panel discussions, or instructions for the distant learners.

Telephone conversations can be used to monitor individual students or to reach numerous students simultaneously via a conference call. Podcast is a method for making digital audio and video files available on the Internet in such a way that others can set their computers to automatically download new episodes in a series as they are posted online.

Concepts and Models

James Taylor's Models of distance education are as follows

The "examination preparation" model

The correspondence education model

The multiple (mass) media model

The group distance education model

The autonomous learner model

The network-based distance teaching model

The technologically extended classroom model

The "examination preparation" model

This model was institutionalized when the University of London was founded in the middle of the 19th century for the benefit of those persons who could not afford to be enrolled at Oxford or Cambridge

University or of those persons who could not attend any university as they lived in the colonies of the British Empire. This university supported the students only by informing them about the examination regulations and sometimes by offering special reading lists. Presently, this model is being developed and practiced by the Regents of the University of New York.

The correspondence education model

This is the oldest and most widely used model. This model is simple and relatively cost-effective since the teaching texts can be mass-produced by the printing press. This model is still used extensively – in spite of the worldwide interest in the digitalization of distance education. It is also used to a great extent by distance teaching universities which take pride in announcing that they are multiple media and open universities.

The multiple (mass) media model

This model was developed in the seventies of our century. Its characteristic feature is the regular and more or less integrated use of radio and television together with printed matter in the form of pre-prepared structured course material. It designates a new era in the development of distance education, namely the second generation of this particular form of academic teaching and learning. It initiated and supported the movement towards open learning and open universities.

The group distance education model

This model is similar to the multiple media model as radio and television are used permanently as teaching media, especially for transporting lectures held by professors. However, these lectures are as a rule not received by individual students but rather by groups of students attending obligatory classes where they follow the explanations of an instructor, discuss what they have heard and watched, do their assignments and take their tests. No special printed teaching material is developed and distributed with the exception of the customary "lecture notes".

The autonomous learner model

This model provides for freedom to develop independent learning. Its goal is the education of the autonomous learner, which is, an ambitious, demanding, but also a very promising goal. The students do not only organize their learning themselves as, e.g., in the correspondence or multiple mass media model, but they tackle also the curricular tasks, they are responsible for determining the aims and objectives, for selecting the contents, for deciding on the strategies and media they want to apply and even for the measurement of their learning success. Here, the long tradition of expository teaching comes to an end.

The network-based distance education model

This model is presently emerging as part of the digital transformation. It provides for the possibility to work in a digitized learning environment. This is a most convenient learning situation. The students have access to even the remotest teaching programmes and databases carrying relevant information. They may work off-line or on-line or use CD-ROMs. They may take part in virtual seminars, workshops, tutorial and counseling meetings, tuition or project groups and chat with their fellow students. The greatest pedagogic advantage, however, is that the students are challenged to develop new forms of learning by searching, finding, acquiring, evaluating, judging, changing, storing, managing and retrieving information when needed. This model is certainly a complex and demanding one. But it is promising as it opens up new dimension of pedagogical endeavour in distance education.

The technologically extended classroom teaching model

This model has been developed in the USA. In this model one teacher teaches a college class or a studio class – and his presentation is transmitted to two or more other classes by cable or satellite TV or with the help of a video conference system. In this way one teacher may teach several classes making the process more economical.

Implementation of ODL

The twentieth century saw the creation and evolution of technologies beyond imagination a century ago. The acceptance of these technologies has led to a new alternative for providing education and training i.e. distance learning. Despite initial concerns that distance learning might lower the quality of instruction, studies show that its benefits are clear and demonstrable and many forms of distance learning are quickly gaining acceptance (Belanger & Jordan, 2000, p. 17).

The implementation of distance learning and its supporting technologies requires careful planning. This process includes four basic steps: conduction of needs assessment, outlining instructional goals and producing instructional materials, providing training and practice for instructors and facilitators and implementing the program.

Conducting the needed assessment includes course, audience instructor and technology analysis. The course analysis is to identify content areas that could be enhanced, through distance learning techniques. Distance learning needs facilitators and technical support teams who will ensure that all equipment is functioning. Instructors, facilitators and technical support staff should be trained for such purpose. Distance learning can be delivered trough different technologies. Selecting the most appropriate technology depends on the content area, student's learning styles and existing hardware and software.

The technology solutions may be impacted by the geographic locations of the teachers and students. A well-structured distance learning course must place instructional objectives foremost. In this case the technology is just another tool that teachers can use to effectively transmit the course content and interact with students.

Once the goals and objectives are outlined, instructional materials can be designed and developed. Materials must be accurate, appropriate and structured to maximize the benefits for students and to minimize the limitations. Teacher training programs are important to acquaint the teachers with the use of technology as well as to help with the re-design of the instructional strategies.

The program can be implemented after the training has been completed and after a pilot test of supporting technologies has been carried out satisfactory. It is important to include structured activities. Timelines, deadlines and feedbacks motivate students and provide the framework students need to function in a flexible environment. The implementation phase should also emphasise interactions. Through the development and implementation, formative evaluation takes place. In selecting distance learning applications factors such as physical location, size and specialization are important for data system creation which supports distance learning.

Conclusion

Distance learning is a contributing force to social and economic development. In developed and developing countries distance education is becoming an essential part of the mainstream of educational systems. The globalization of distance learning provides many opportunities for countries for the realization of their education system-wide goals. The growing needs for continual skills upgrading and retraining and the technological advances have led to an explosion of interest in distance learning.

Reference

1. Ashok K Gaba, Professor, IGNOU, Global Skills Summit 2011 presentation.
2. Bates A.W, The impact of Technological change in IDL: In Distance Education 1997, Vol 18, p. 93-109.
3. Madhava Menon Report on ODL, 2010.
4. Saima Ghosh, Journal of Global Research in Computer Science, April 2012, p.53-57.
5. Viplav Baxi, Report on ODL in India, April 14, 2012.
6. UGC Annual Report 2010 – 2011.
7. www.mhrd.gov.in.
8. http://www.c3l.uni-oldenburg.de/cde/found/peter98b.htm
9. http://www.slideshare.net/missan/open-and-distance-learning-history-status-and-trends.

20

Blended Learning in Teacher Education

Introduction

Educator's seem to have the most interest in blended learning, gives learners and teachers a potential environment to learn and teach more effectively than any other method of teaching. Because of this much of the research on blended learning has been based around classroom situations. All levels of education have been researched width blended learning; from the elementary school grades up to graduate school Educator's interests in blended learning are common to most effective and efficient teachers.

Blended learning provides a 'good mix of technologies and interactions, resulting in a socially supported,constructive,learning experience, this is especially a significant given the profound effect that it could have on teacher education learning.

Objectives

1. To understand the different approaches to Blended learning.
2. To attain knowledge of the various models of teaching

3. The institutional capacity available at present for all levels of school education
4. Understand the different components levels of teaching
5. The teacher face while designing a blended learning is to determine the balance between online and face to face instruction.

Blended Learning

A blended learning approach combines face to face classroom methods. A thoughtfully designed. Integration of live and online materials and methods in the post digital materials have served in a supplementary role helping to support face to face instruction for students of all ages and levels of learning. The best aspects of online instruction students in advanced interactive experiences. mean while, the online portion of the course can provide students with multimedia rich content at any time of day anywhere the students has internet access from computer labs. This allows for an increase in scheduling flexibility for students, hence it is necessary for the educators to utilize the Blended learning approach in teaching learning process to be more effective for classroom instruction.

1. The institution enhance under enrolled programs, computer faculty teaching loads.
2. Blended learning across the curriculum by blending the boundaries of knowledge.
3. Creative thinking processes are developed within a meaningful context in lifelong earning
4. Students can participate at any time
5. Class goals can easily to meet.
6. Increase the quality of communication between the instructor and learner.

Technology in Blended Learning

Technology in education leads to achieve a milestone in the field of education like Self learning

1. Life-long education

2. Learning at one's own convenience and choice
3. Multimedia learning

Models of Blended Learning

Blended learning can be group into models based on the difference in teacher roles. Physical space delivery methods and scheduling the models of blended learning are,

1. Face to face driver
2. Online lab
3. Self-Blend
4. Online communications
5. Flex
6. Rotation
7. Self faced learning
8. Online driver

Benefits of Blended Learning

1. Blended learning combines online and classroom learning activities and resources to reduce in-class seat time for students in a face to face learning
2. It can be a tremendous for a university
3. Multiple learning sources
4. Equal opportunity to obtain education and information
5. Promote technology literacy of all students
6. Many more innovation in teaching and learning methodology.

Importance of Blended learning

Learning quite different for each learner in that we have to consider differences in

1. Importance of aptitudes
2. Interest spans

3. Preservation of knowledge
4. Creation of interesting learning situation
5. Achievements and motivation

Conclusion

The Blended learning approach used consists of face to face instruction, from textbooks and developed teacher education is one of the special professional courses designed for the post higher graduate students learning. The study involving the blended learning approach has shown that students demonstrate positive perceptions towards learning.

A blended learning should describe a planned and deliberate educational activity that integrate students-centered learning classroom based teaching and learning based on individual learners and their specific needs.

References

1. http://www.kneulton.com/blended-learning/
2. http://www.blended learning now.com/
3. http://en.wikipedia.org/wiki/blended learning
4. http:\\weblearning.PSU.edu/blended-learning initiative/ blended learning.

21

An Assessment of Edu Digital Skills of Teachers in Namakkal District

Introduction

Teacher is an ideal personality whose knowledge and skill play a major role in the development of the nation to the global standard education in general and tapping the potentialities of students to the maximum extent in particular. Teachers are expected to learn forever to withstand the innovations in teaching and updating the knowledge and widen the clarity of the conceptual framework of the subject of specialization too. Unless and until the teachers prepared to meet the requirements and challenges, the dream and purpose of education will not be fulfilled. Nowadays the system of education has assumed the character which involves more students' participation and student centric which is highly enabled through the application of various educational technologies. Edu - digital skills is considered prerequisite for all teachers teaching for nursery to doctorate scholars. 21st century school curriculum has been enriched to meet the demands of world requirements of quality. Communication, collaboration, critical thinking, problem solving, creativity, invention, information and technology literacy and self direction will facilitate the achievement of aims and objectives of education. Teachers of 21st century are expected to equip themselves with modern technology application in teaching and learning process. A paradigm shift has happened to meet the demands of gen y and z learners which require innovative, explorative and interesting approach in teaching and learning. The curriculum will need withstand the futuristic vision for the global scenario. At this juncture the teachers of today should be enthusiastic to update their knowledge and skills forever in order to keep young to the youngest generation whom they meet and it may also be emphasized greatly as the professional ethics. This study has been attempted to assess the knowledge and skills of teachers in the field of information and communication technology which a teacher necessarily possess in the digital world.

Teacher is an ideal personality whose knowledge and skill play a major role in the development of the nation to the global standard education in general and tapping the potentialities of students to the maximum extent in particular. Teachers are expected to learn forever to withstand the innovations in teaching and updating the knowledge and widen the clarity of the conceptual framework of the subject of specialization too. Unless and until the teachers prepared to meet the requirements and challenges, the dream and purpose of education will not be fulfilled. Nowadays the system of education has assumed the character which involves more students' participation and student centric which is highly enabled through the application of various educational technologies. Edu - digital skills is considered prerequisite for all teachers teaching for nursery to doctorate scholars. 21st century school curriculum has been enriched to meet the demands of world requirements of quality. Communication, collaboration, critical thinking, problem solving, creativity, invention, information and technology literacy and self direction will facilitate the achievement of aims and objectives of education. Teachers of 21st century are expected to equip themselves with modern technology application in teaching and learning process. A paradigm shift has happened to meet the demands of gen y and z learners which require innovative, explorative and interesting approach in teaching and learning. The curriculum will need withstand the futuristic vision for the global scenario. At this juncture the teachers of today should be enthusiastic to update their knowledge and skills forever in order to keep young to the youngest generation whom they meet and it may also be emphasized greatly as the professional ethics. This study has been attempted to assess the knowledge and skills of teachers in the field of information and communication technology which a teacher necessarily possess in the digital world.

Educational Digital Skills

It is mentioned that in order to thrive in a digital economy, students will need digital age proficiencies. It is important for the educational system to make parallel changes in order to fulfill its mission in society, namely the preparation of students for the world beyond the classroom. Therefore, the educational system must understand and embrace the following 21st century skills within the context of rigorous academic standards.

The 21st Century Literacy Summit (2002) contends that "the explosive growth of technology in every aspect of society offers us a unique opportunity to engage our citizens in economic and civic life" The report further states that to take advantage of this opportunity, we must continually acquire and develop new knowledge and skills. Summit participants noted "Information and communication technologies are raising the bar on the competencies needed to succeed in the 21st century, and they are compelling us to revisit many of our assumptions and beliefs" The sheer magnitude of human knowledge, world to technology necessitates a shift in our children's education - from plateaus of knowing to continuous cycles of learning. Therefore, policymakers and educators alike must define 21st century skills, highlighting the relationship of those skills to conventional academic standards. As they do so, they must also recognize the need for multiple assessments to measure these skills within the context of academic standards, evaluating their application to today's technological and global society.

Technological Literacy

Demonstrate a sound conceptual understanding of the nature of technology systems and view themselves as proficient users of these systems. Understand and model positive, ethical use of technology in both social and personal contexts. Use a variety of technology tools in effective ways to increase creative productivity. Use communication tools to reach out to the world beyond the classroom and communicate ideas in powerful ways. Use technology effectively to access, evaluate, process and synthesize information from a variety of sources. Use technology to identify and solve complex problems in real-world contexts have been considered as Technological Literacy.

Information Literacy

Before Accessing Information one should determine what is known and what is needed for problem solving, identify different sources of information, including text, people, video, audio, and databases and prioritize sources based on credibility and relevance. When Accessing Information one need identify and retrieve relevant information from sources and use technology to enhance searching. Revise information-gathering strategies that prove to be in effective when understands how information retrieved does or does not address original problem, evaluate information in terms of credibility and know what are the social, economic, political, legal, and ethical issues that may impact it to facilitate to use technology for evaluation. After Information is extracted, using retrieved information to accomplish a specific purpose, present information clearly and persuasively by using a range of technology tools and media and evaluate the processes and products of these activities have here been considered essential to assure one to be Literate in information.

Global Awareness

Global awareness is knowledge about the connectedness of the nations of the world historically, politically, economically, technologically, socially, linguistically, and ecologically and understand that these interconnections of positive benefits and negative consequences too. The ability to recognize, analyzes, and evaluates major trends in global relations and the interconnections of these trends with both their local and national communities. Participate in the global society by staying current with international news and by participating in the democratic process.

Objectives of the Study

To find the level of Edu-digital skill among school teachers and find whether there is significant different exist among them in relation to their personal variables such as sex, Age, Educational Qualification, Area of Residence, Management of the Institution, Subject of Specialization and the Location of the School.

Research Question

What is the level of educational digital Skills of School Teachers? Is there any Significant Difference Exists among them with respect to their Personal Variables?

Research Methodology

A Normative Descriptive Method of study has been attempted to assess the level of Educational Digital Skills among the School Teachers in Namakkal District.

Population, Sample and Sampling Technique of the Study

All teachers who teach in school education are the population of the study and the sample of the study has been chosen from teachers work in Namakkal district only and the sample was taken by stratified random sampling technique which consists of 250.

Tools and Technique of Data Collection

A tool consisted of 24 items related to some basic skills necessary for adopting computer enabled teaching technology, using internet connection which will benefit students to gain knowledge, understand the concept better, improve the critical thinking, problem solving ability, creativity and to enhance their communication skill and appropriate application of the knowledge gained for the betterment of himself and to the society. The scope of this study extent all teachers who teach in the classroom from kindergarten to plus two levels. The questionnaire has dimensions of using the computer for retrieving useful information via internet, knowledge about various search engines, and preparation of effective PowerPoint materials, video clippings, software package application, audio recording, connecting to virtual classroom and the facilities to publish the students works in internet. Knowledge and the application of MS word, Excel format, mobile for teaching and learning purpose and the ability to set ready LCD, mike and arrange show in the smart classroom and the application of social media in education have also been taken for assessing.

Scoring Procedure & Statistical Tools Used

The Questionnaire used in the study has five point scale of the level of skill of the respondents in relation to their digital skill hence it has five options of known very well, known, moderately known, known little and Unknown which scored as 5, 4,3,2 and 1 respectively.

SPSS package has been used to analyze the data and the percentage analysis and the differential analysis have been used to describe and infer the details pertaining to the research question formulated for the study.

Table -1

An Analysis of Edu Digital Skills among Teachers in Namakkal District

Items	Very well Known		Well Known		Moderately Known		Known Little		Unknown		Total
	F	%	F	%	F	%	F	%	F	%	
Information Retrieval	41	16.4	59	23.6	62	24.8	75	30	13	5.2	250
Power point preparation	52	20.8	67	26.8	53	21.2	60	24	18	7.2	250
Efficient use of Windows operating system	35	14	48	19.2	75	30	81	32.4	11	4.4	250
Connecting to the Online Teaching of World Classroom	15	6	20	8	39	15.6	116	46.4	60	24	250
Skill in make it work well of LCD mike screen view	15	6	26	10.4	77	30.8	114	45.6	18	7.2	250
Knowledge about E learning material preparation	21	8.4	15	6	27	10.8	129	51.6	58	23.2	250
Account in social networking sites like	22	8.8	36	14.4	74	29.6	12	4.8	106	42.4	250

Face-book, twitter											
Using of videos and computer games in teaching	19	7.6	29	11.6	55	22	85	34	62	24.8	250
Application of Virtual classrooms and chat rooms in teaching and learning	13	5.2	18	7.2	17	6.8	56	22.4	146	58.4	250
Application of documentary film in deliverance of the instructional objectives	51	20.4	60	24	41	16.4	31	12.4	67	26.8	250
Using of web- Camera in virtual interaction	16	6.4	41	16.4	27	10.8	71	28.4	95	38	250
Application of white Board in teaching	25	10	16	6.4	19	7.6	43	17.2	147	58.8	250
Safety and security issues in using webmail	17	6.8	39	15.6	90	36	70	28	44	17.6	250
Security Challenges in instant messaging	15	6	35	14	78	31.2	98	39.2	24	9.6	250
Application of iPod and tables in teaching	11	4.4	23	9.2	67	26.8	80	32	69	27.6	250
Application of Video conferencing for teaching and learning	32	12.8	24	9.6	71	28.4	90	36	33	13.2	250
Application of YouTube	49	19.6	86	34.4	55	22	62	24.8	38	15.2	250
Application of Flicker & Picasa	19	7.6	25	10	62	24.8	104	41.6	40	16	250
Application of mobile phone for transferring data of video	21	8.4	27	10.8	80	32	90	36	32	12.8	250
Application of mobile phone for transferring data of voice	22	8.8	33	13.2	76	30.4	81	32.4	38	15.2	250
Application of mobile phone for transferring data of text	187	74.8	46	18.4	3	1.2	9	3.6	5	2	250
Assessment of students performance through online	25	10	52	20.8	58	23.2	105	42	10	4	250
Application of learning Management System - LMS	11	4.4	21	8.4	37	14.8	57	22.8	15	6	250
Application of Video -recording	17	6.8	26	10.4	51	20.4	78	31.2	78	31.2	250

Majority of teachers have necessary in Skill and knowledge in the application of MS office, Mobile technology in teaching and learning, information retrieval system from online resource centre but the majority teachers have moderate and least knowledge about e-content preparation, application of social media, and security issues in web mails, various learning management system and efficient use of ICT in teaching

Table -2

Significance of Difference in Edu-Digital Skill of Teachers

Demographic Variables	P Value	Level of Sig.
Sex	0.153	NS
Area of Residence	0.104	NS
Location of the School	0.214	NS
Teaching Experience	0.098	NS
Educational Qualification	0.521	NS
Management of the School	0.021*	S
Subject of Specialization	0.001**	S

There is no significant difference exist among the respondents in their Educational digital skill in relation to their personal variables of Sex, Area of Residence, Location of the School, Teaching Experience and their educational qualification. But the statistical report of analysis shows that there is significant difference exist among the sample in relation to their management of the school and their subject of specialization.

Educational Implications

1. Teacher Education curriculum should emphasize the ICT enabled education in B.Ed program
2. Workshops need to be conducted for B.Ed program in the practical application of ICT and training program can be organized for E- content preparation
3. Orientation and Refresher courses for the teachers in schools should be conducted frequently to enable teachers to facilitate them in the efficient use of ICT in teaching and learning environment
4. Collaborative Approach should be made in integrating ICT in education

Conclusion

Teachers are the forerunner of all developments and growth of the nation and the world; they play a significant role in bringing desirable outcome in the world with their adaptability and their ever learning behavior of updating knowledge and skills in any field. No technology can replace the teacher in any period of time but the teacher needs possess skills in the application of technology which facilitate desirable educational outcome in the field of education.

References

1. Felix.A & Jahitha Begum (2011) "An Awareness of E-resources related to ICT and Education among M.Ed Students and M.Phil Scholars" ICT in teaching and learning, APH Publishing Corporation, New Delhi, p.169
2. Nagarajan .K (2009) "Educational Innovations and Management" Ram Publishers, Chennai. Pp.135-185.
3. Natchimuthu.K (2012), "Need of E-Content Development in Education Today" APH Publication Corporation, New Delhi. P.76.
4. Rangarajan. P & Senthilnathan.S (2012) "Teacher Educators Attitude towards E Learning" Edutracks, Vol.No.12 No.1 pp. 21-32.
5. www.educatorstechnology.com/2012/06/33-digital-skills-every-21st-century.htm
6. http://www.educatorstechnology.com/2013/07/the-8-digital-skills-students-need-for.html

22

Creative Society and Generating Employability

Introduction

"'Creating Learning without Limits' takes on one of the most important issues in education today. In the last decade schools in have taken a path towards putting all children into boxes, attaching a level to their heads and deciding what they are capable of achieving. The possibility of a different educational path, one in which all students are encouraged to achieve the greatest they can. Importantly the book also documents ways in which courageous teachers can do this - promoting fair and engaging learning environments for all students. This is a must-read for educators, policy makers and parents alike.""This will undoubtedly turn out to be amongst the most important educational books of the decade. Our capacity to respond, both individually and collectively, to its key insights and messages will profoundly affect not just the quality of our schools, but of our society for years to come. It reminds us why people come into education - to make a difference for children. To make a deep difference we have to organize education differently. It describes a school that vibrates with learning in an atmosphere of deep humanity and care. Its practices are light years away from the measuring, labeling, targeting, and testing structures that have become our recent national norm. The school as a whole community transforms people."

"The self-confidence that comes from a profound faith in the capacity of every child to be a passionate and engaged learner. This in the face of powerful and societal dominant messages that explicitly or more insidiously tell a different and more deterministic tale: that children (and schools) are fit and proper subjects for classification, measurement and management. And there's more - the careful scholarship on which this story is based prevents this book from being merely a description of what happens when a unique constellation of propitious circumstances meets a charismatic leader: this 'other way' is open to all who will take it - but it will demand the laying of solid and value-rich foundations, the exercising of autonomy for staff and pupils, the rethinking of relationships, a focus on learning (letting performance come as a secondary gift), and the taking of collective action. It's become a cliché to say of a book that it 'should be read by every teacher (or parent, or whoever ...).' This one, and its predecessor 'Learning withoutLimits"meritsthatinjunction."

"Creating Learning without Limits provides a welcome tonic that can help to offset the beleaguering effects of a performativity and standards agenda that reinforces the ability based practices so pervasive in schools today. Building on the compelling pedagogy first presented in 'Learning without Limits', this inspiring book shows how an alternative school improvement agenda can produce high academic attainment and enhanced capacity to learn for everybody. A classic for our time, it should be read by all who seek approaches to teaching and learning that are free from externally imposed views of ability and potential."

Professor Lain Florien, School of Education, University of Aberdeen, UK

That human potential is not predictable, that child's futures are unknowable, and that education has the power to enhance the lives of all', read the book! You will however need to proceed with caution; it will make some of you reflect on what you do and why you are doing it. This book could be the catalyst for the educational change that we are allprayingfor." Many students would likely cite a desire to learn. Students assume that, because they have read their text and memorized facts, they have learned something. Definition of 'learn' in a dictionary step, Step1. To acquire knowledge of a subject or skill through education or experience, Step2. To gain information about somebody or something. Step3. To memorize something. This definition is not particularly insightful, although it reminds us that the word can be used to describe the acquisition of both knowledge and skill, and that acquisition can be by a variety of means. Including education experience, or memorization.

The Current Situation

The American education system is considered among the best in the world. More than 50% of our nation's high school graduates continue on to college and each year our universities and colleges enroll thousands of students from other countries. Despite these statistics, several recent studies have shown that many college seniors have neither good general knowledge nor the necessary skills for reasoning in today's society. At the end of the course, the test scores of those students who had completed the economics course were only 20% better than those who had not taken the course, and this difference dropped to less than 10% seven years after completion of the course. The results and many others, strongly suggest that our current instructional practices are not working and that many students are not learning, or retaining what they do learn.

Need for New Kinds of Learning

There have been calls for new kinds of learning from many different parts of society. College teachers have expressed frustration about attendance in class, uncompleted reading assignments, and students focus on grades rather than learning. Student surveys indicate that courses are not interesting, that students fail to recognize the value of what they are learning, and that many faculty rely too heavily on lectures for transmitting information. The 1996

National Science Foundation report on shaping the future urges faculty to promote new kinds of learning that include developing skills in communication, teamwork, and lifelong learning. Gardiner(1994) compiled a list of critical competencies for citizens and workers from leaders in business, industry and government.

1. Personal responsibility.
2. Ability to act in principled, ethical fashion
3. Skill in oral and written communication
4. Interpersonal and team skills
5. Skills in critical thinking and problem-solving
6. Respect for people different from oneself,
7. Ability to change
8. Ability and desire for lifelong learning.

Society and individual learners now have different needs, both in terms of what people need to learn and how they can and should learn. It is a great nuisance that knowledge can be acquired only by hard work-Somerset Maugham.

Implement learning strategies and evaluate learning outcomes

Effectively communicate orally, visually in writing and in a second language. Understand and employ Quantitative and Qualitative analysis to solve problems.

Intellectual Skills

The human imagination, expression, and the products of many cultures. Means of modeling the natural, social and technical words

Different kinds of thinking and learning

In cognitive theory and education have used Bloom's (1956) taxonomic of learning. Bloom and colleagues identified three learning domains. The cognitive domains involve thinking of all sorts. The affective domain includes feelings, emotions, attitude, values and motivations.

The psychomotor domain of learning includes physical movement, coordination, motor, and sensory-skills. When a learning experience has a profound effect on a student, it can result in a greater sense of caring for the subject, for them, other or learning in general. Greater caring can lead to new interests, energy for learning, or a change in values. 'To learn how to learn' this includes learning how to diagnose one's own need for learning and how to be a self-learner. Then type of learning enables students to continue learning with greater effectiveness and is a particularly important skill with the recent explosion of knowledge and technology.

Learning and the Brain

Many people both young and old enjoy solving problems. These observation suggest that the human brain has a fundamental need to solve problems and understand its surroundings. New understanding of the working of the brain.

1. Learning changes the physical structure of the brain.
2. Learning organized and reorganizes the brain.
3. Different parts of the brain may be ready to learn at different stages of development.

   Experience equate to learning, the brain is a dynamic organ. Learning in individual and social contexts actually results in new pattern of organization and improved functioning of the brain.

Intellectual development

One goal of college education should be to develop more sophisticated approaches to thinking.

1. Dualism (authority)
2. Multiplicity (opinion)
3. Relativism (perspective)
4. Commitment (understanding)

Critical Thinking

"A tool for everyone" Critical thinking is so central to sound reasoning that it deserves special attention. The methods of critical thought arc by no means limited to thinking in science, but have also been applied in virtually all other disciplines. They involve both cognitive and affective components.

Critical thinking is the intellectually disciplined process of actively and skillfully conceptualizing, applying, analyzing, synthesizing and evaluating information gathered from or generated by observation experience, reflection, reasoning or communication as a guide to belief and action.

National Council for Excellence in Critical Thinking, Paul and Elder(2004)

1) Be able to identify the parts of their thinking and 2) be able to assess their use of those parts in thinking. Paul and Elder suggest the following elements of critical thinking:

9. All reasoning has a purpose
10. All reasoning is an attempt to figure something out, to settle some question, to solve some problem
11. All reasoning is based on assumptions
12. All reasoning is done from some point of view
13. All reasoning is based on data, information and evidence
14. All reasoning is expressed through, and shaped by concepts and ideas
15. All reasoning contains inferences by which we draw conclusions and give meaning
16. All reasoning leads somewhere, has implications and consequence.

The elements of one's reasoning can be assessed using standards such as clarity, precision, accuracy, relevance, depth, breadth, logic, and significance.

Thinking about one's own Thinking and Learning

Intentional thought about one's own thinking is generally regarded as an essential component of successful thinkers and learners monitor their understanding and progress during problem solving.

I went to a bookstore and asked the sales-woman, "Where's the self-help section?" She said if she told me, it would defeat the purpose-George Carlin

Effective Learning and Learning Styles

Best learning occurs when students are engaged in active learning- when they are doing things instead of sitting passively and listening. In a recent review of the effectiveness of active learning, Prince (2004) found extensive, widespread support for active learning approaches, especially when activities were designed around important learning outcomes and promoted thoughtful engagement. Many instructors recognize that active learning results in significant improvements in student knowledge retention, conceptual understanding, engagement, and attitudes about learning.

A commonly used approach in active learning is cooperative learning. An enormous body of research confirms the effectiveness of cooperative learning. Compared with more traditional individualized and competitive models of learning, students who learn in cooperative groups exhibit markedly improved individual achievement.

Conclusion

There are many different ways of modeling the way of learning. No one model provides a complete description of learning, and no single learning style is superior to another. However, it is important to be aware of your own learning style preferences so that you can make the necessary adjustments to maximize your learning. Unfamiliar pedagogies example active learning, cooperative learning. These have largely been designed to teach to a wide variety of learning styles and to facilitate learning the content and skills encompassed within significant learning. Some of these new instructional approaches keep an open mind and try to understand the objectives of each pedagogical approach. If you have questions about classroom methods, ask your instructor. Most teachers are happy to discuss instructional practices with their students.

Bibliography

1. AACU,2002, Greater Expectations: A New Vision for Learning as a Nation Goes to College: National panel Report, American Association of Colleges and Universities, Washington,DC62p.
2. Atkinson,R.L Atkinson R.C Smith, E.E and Bem D.J., 1993, Introduction to Psychology, Harcourt Brace Jovanovich, Fort Worth, TX, 11 the edition
3. Cuesta College, 2004, Characteristics of a Successful Student: Cuesta College. Available at: http://academic. Cuesta.edu/accasupp/as/201.HTM.
4. Johnson, D.W., Johnson, R.T., and Smith, K., 1991,Active Learning: Cooperation in the College Classroom Interaction Book Company,Edina,MN.
5. Krathwohl, D.R.Bloom, B.S, and Masia,B.B., 1964, Taxonomy of Educational objectives. The classification of Educational Goals, Handbook II: Affective Domain. David McKay Company,Inc
6. Teaching Goals Inventory,2004, Available form: http://www.uiowa.edu/-centeach/tgi/.
7. Williams,John,H., 1993, Clarifying grade expectations. The Teaching Professor, August/September.

23

Essential Technology Concepts and Digital Skills For High School Students

Introduction

This paper analyzes the effects of increased shared computer access in secondary schools in Tirupati. Administrative data are used to identify, through propensity-score matching, two groups of schools with similar observable educational inputs but different intensity in computer access. Extensive primary data collected from the 20 matched schools are used to determine whether increased shared computer access at schools affects digital skills and academic achievement. Results suggest that small increases in shared computer access, one more computer per 40 students, can produce large increases in digital skills (0.3 standard deviations). No effects are found on test scores in Math and Language. This paper examines whether moderate increases in school computer access affect students' digital skills. Additionally, we assess effects on test scores in Math and Language.

The methodology exploits cross-sectional variation in computer access across secondary schools. This variation might be correlated with a host of important variables, raising the possibility of biased estimates.

Governments around the world are making large investments in technology in education programs. There is mounting research on the effects of these programs on learning in core subjects such as Math and Language (Cheung and Slavin, 2013)[1]. However, many programs are mainly intended to develop students' digital skills, that is, on preparing students to effectively use technology in their lives. Public programs that provide one personal laptop to each student have shown sizable positive effects on digital skills (Malamud and Pop-Eleches, 2011; Mo et al., 2012)[2-3]. However, these programs might be too costly for many countries. Alternatively, providing shared computer access at schools might give students sufficient technology exposure at a fraction of the cost. Yet, there is little evidence of the effects of such less expensive programs on the development of digital skills. There is an emerging literature documenting the effects of expanding computer access on digital skills. As noted, the available literature has analyzed the effects of programs that have provided personal computers to students. Fairlie (2012)[4] studies the impact of a program for college students and finds a 17 percentage point increase in self-reported computer mastery. Malamud and Pop-Eleches (2011)[5] estimate that a program that provided vouchers for the purchase of computers in Romania improved digital skills by 0.25 standard deviations. Mo et al. (2012)[6] evaluate the impact of a program in China for primary students and find an impact of 0.33 standard deviations on computer skills. Beuermann et al. (2012)[7] found an impact of 0.88 standard deviations on skills specific to the use of the OLPC laptop but no effects on skills associated with Windows or Internet use.

Technology in Public Secondary Schools

There had been limited efforts to promote technology access and use in public schools in Tirupati. Between 1996 and 2001, several small-scale independent programs, mainly targeting secondary schools were launched. These programs funded some technology resources (hardware, software, training and support) and required some investments from participating schools to be included in the program. These investments were typically funded by parents, private donations or other (non-public) sources of funding. This requirement promoted ownership and sustainability of the investment but at the expense of poor targeting (large public urban schools in more affluent areas received more resources). In this context, computers were mainly used for acquiring digital skills, for browsing the web, and for communication purposes.

The objective is to increase the quality of the education sector by incorporating the use of technology in the learning process. The program mainly targeted secondary schools although some primary schools were also covered. Schools selected into the program received hardware, software (Microsoft Office applications and digital media but not interactive software) and teacher training, and they were prioritized to receive Internet access. Innovation room coordinators are to be assigned to schools. These individuals, trained in information technology and pedagogy, were responsible for ensuring the effective use of computer labs in subject areas. They were also expected to organize training sessions in the schools to contribute to the development of subject teachers' and principals' digital skills. This structure suggests that the program sought to incorporate the use of computers into core-subject teaching and not just enhance computer skills.

Three factors are considered to select the final set of schools: i) high enrollment levels, ii) ease of access to schools, iii) commitment by principals, teachers and parents to support and sustain the initiative. Still, other factors may have been considered. Between 2006 and 2008 (the period relevant to this study) there was little policy action on technology in education in secondary schools as the government shifted its efforts to implement the One Laptop per Child program in primary schools in rural areas.

Essential Technology Concepts and Skills

The essential technology concepts and skills needed for the education of high school children are discussed below.

(1) Demonstration of creative thinking, construct knowledge and develop innovative products and processes using technology.

Apply existing knowledge to generate new ideas, products, or processes.

- Students design, develop, create, and/or test self-generated digital learning objects that are accessible by as many users as possible, and demonstrate knowledge and skills related to curriculum content. Create original works as a means of personal or group expression.
- Students individually or collaboratively create media-rich products to be displayed, published, or performed for a variety of audiences. Use models and simulations to explore complex systems and issues.
- Students employ curriculum-specific, technology-based simulations to aid them in understanding complex, real-world systems. Simulation studies include formulating problems, developing models, running models, and analyzing outputs that help predict behaviours and outcomes. Identify trends and forecast possibilities.
- Students investigate complex global issues, make informed choices based on capabilities and limitations of technology systems, resources, and services, and apply this learning to personal and workplace needs.

(2) Use digital media and environments to communicate and work collaboratively, including at a distance, to support individual learning and contribute to the learning of others. Interact, collaborate, and publish with peers, experts, or others employing a variety of digital environments and media.

- Using technology, students interact and collaborate with peers, experts, and others to contribute to a content-related, media-rich knowledge base by compiling, synthesizing, producing, and disseminating information, models, and other creative works. Communicate information and ideas effectively to multiple audiences using a variety of media and formats.
- Students use technology tools and resources, including distance and distributededucation for effectively exchanging information with a variety of audiences in an array of media-

rich formats. Develop cultural understanding and global awareness by engaging with learners of other cultures.

- Students use a variety of existing online tools and emerging technologies for communicating with and learning about people of other cultures. Students investigate, communicate and understand cultural norms manifested in music, literature, painting and sculpture, and theater and film, resulting in greater global awareness. Appropriately contribute to project teams to produce original works or solve problems.
- Students share knowledge and skills with local or distance teams of peers, experts, orothers using technological tools and resources to create collaborative works and/or innovative sustainable solutions.

(3) Understand human, cultural, and societal issues related to technology and practice legal and ethical behaviour.

Advocate and practice safe, legal, and responsible use of information and technology at an appropriate level.

- Students use technology efficiently and in a manner that does not harm them or others. Their choices demonstrate and advocate for legal and ethical behaviors among peers, family, and community regarding the use of technology and information. Students understand the concept of acceptable use of copyrighted materials, and how disregarding intellectual property affects others.

Exhibit a positive attitude toward using technology that supports collaboration, learning, and productivity.

- Students willingly and routinely use online resources to meet needs for collaboration, research, publication, communication, and productivity. Evidence for a positive attitude includes a proclivity to help others with the use of technology in their learning.

Demonstrate personal responsibility for lifelong learning.

- Students use their skills to identify capabilities and limitations of contemporary and emerging technology resources and assess the potential of these systems and services to address personal, lifelong learning, and workplace needs. They use this knowledge to make informed choices among technology systems, resources, and services.

- Students use their skills to identify capabilities and limitations of contemporary and emerging technology resources and assess the potential of these systems and services to address personal, lifelong learning, and workplace needs. They use this knowledge to make informed choices among technology systems, resources, and services.

(4) Essential Concept and/or Skill: Demonstrate a sound understanding of technology concepts, systems and operations.

Understand and use technology systems

- Students adapt to evolving technology systems and apply them for everyday use. They, also interpret the underlying structure of the system so it can be used for multiple purposes and applied to unique situations.

Select and use applications effectively and productively,

- Students select and apply technology tools for research, information analysis, problem solving, and decision-making. Students use technology tools and resources for managing and communicating personal and professional information (e.g. finances, schedules, addresses, purchases, correspondence).

Troubleshoot systems and applications.

- Students utilize a working knowledge of technology or technological support services to identify a problem/issue and its solution.

Transfer current knowledge to learning of new technologies.

- Students apply what they know of one technology to intuitively utilize other technologies.

Conclusion

This paper studies whether increases in technology inputs in secondary schools in Peru translate into more hours of use of these resources in Math, Language and technology and into learning in these areas. To this end, we applied matching techniques to rich administrative census data for public urban schools to generate two sets of schools that are different in technology access but similar on observable educational inputs. Next, we collected primary data on these schools and verified that the empirical strategy followed achieved both stated objectives. Schools in the treatment group have more than double the number of computers than the comparison group (23 versus 11), increased Internet access (24 percentage points) and increased availability of computer labs and technology coordinators (20 and 27 percentage points, respectively). We also document that important characteristics at the student, teacher and principal levels are well balanced across groups.

We found that increased access to computers in the treatment group translated into increases in time used to teach digital skills, but no increases are found in computer time devoted to Math and Language. Consistent with the findings on use, we find no impacts for Math and Spanish but large effects on digital skills. The estimated impacts are sufficiently large to more than compensate for reductions in test scores in technology associated with not having a computer at home before entering secondary school, being female or having a mother with less than high school.

References

1. Cheung, A. and R. Slavin (2013). "The Effectiveness of Educational Technology Applications for Enhancing Mathematics Achievement in K-12 Classrooms: A Meta-Analysis." Education Research Review 9: 88-113.
2. Malamud, O. and C. Pop-Eleches (2011). "Home Computer Use and the Development of Human Capital." Quarterly Journal of Economics 126: 987-1027.
3. Mo, D. (2013). "Can One-to-One Computing Narrow the Digital Divide and the Educational Gap in China? The Case of Beijing Migrant Schools", World Development 46: 14-29.
4. Fairlie, R. (2012). "The Effects of Home Access to Technology on Computer Skills: Evidence from a Field Experiment." Information Economics and Policy 24: 243-253.

5. Malamud, O. and C. Pop-Eleches (2011). Ibid.

6. Mo, D. (2013) Ibid.

7. Beuermann, D. 2012. "Home Computers and Child Outcomes: Short-Term Impacts from a Randomized Experiment in Peru", Working Paper IDB WP-382, Washington, DC, United States: Inter-American Development Bank.

8. Malamud, O. and C. Pop-Eleches (2011). Ibid.

9. Linden, L. (2008)."Complement or Substitute? The Effect of Technology on Students Achievement in India", New York, United States: Columbia University, Mimeographed document.

24

Reversal of Traditional Teaching

Introduction

The flipped classroom describes a reversal of traditional teaching where students gain first exposure to new material outside of class, usually via reading or lecture videos, and then class time is used to do the harder work of assimilating that knowledge through strategies such as problem-solving, discussion or debates.

The purpose of flipping the classroom is to shift from passive to active learning to focus on the higher order thinking skills such as analysis, synthesis and evaluation (Bloom). As explained in this short video, flipping the Classroom: Simply Speaking (Penn State), student access key content individually (or in small groups) prior to class time and then meet face-to-face in the larger group to explore content through active learning and engagement strategies.

There are many permutations of what a flipped classroom will look like and depends on variables such as class size, resources, support and readiness to change. At several teachers across the faculties have already flipped their classrooms and their valuable experiences have been captured in the Studies section.

In the flipped classroom, the roles and expectations of students and teachers change where:

- students take more responsibility for their own learning and study core content either individually or in groups before class and then apply knowledge and skills to a range of activities using higher order thinking,
- Teaching 'one-to-many' focuses more on facilitation and moderation than lecturing, though lecturing is still important. Significant learning opportunities can be gained through facilitating active learning, engaging students, guiding learning, correcting misunderstandings and providing timely feedback using a variety of pedagogical strategies, there is a greater focus on concept exploration, meaning making and demonstration or application of knowledge in the face-to-face setting

What is flipping?

Flipping the classroom is a "pedagogy-first" approach to teaching. In this approach in-class time is "re-purposed" for inquiry, application, and assessment in order to better meet the needs of the individual learners. Students gain control of the learning process through studying course material outside of class, using readings, pre-recorded video lectures, or research assignments. During class time, instructors become facilitators of the learning process by helping students work through problems individually and in groups.

Over the past few years, the flipped classroom model has really taken off in classrooms around the world. This model of teaching and learning has proved to be incredibly valuable to both teachers and students. It allows teachers to spend more time working with their students in the classroom, while allowing students to take control of their own learning and work at a pace that is most comfortable to them. It also provides ample opportunities for students to engage in hands-on activities and meaningful learning both in and out of the classroom. The flipped classroom model not only fosters the development of 21st century skills, but also creates an any time, any place, any pace learning environment for students.

Why change? Flipping

Speaks the language of today's students

1. Helps busy students
2. Helps struggling students
3. Helps students of all abilities excel
4. Allow students to pause and rewind their teacher
5. Increase student- teacher interaction
6. Allows teachers to know their students better
7. Educates not only students but parents and other siblings

Flipping for Mastery

Mastery Learning enables students to take responsibility for their own learning. Mastery Learning allows students to work at their own pace through the curriculum. Students conduct experiments, watch podcasts, work on assignments, interact with the class learning management site, have one-on-one discussions with their teacher, and get tutored by their peers and cadet teachers. When they complete a unit they must demonstrate that they have learned the content by taking an exit assessment that includes both a project and an exam. If students score less than 85% on these exit assessments, they must go back and re-learn those concepts they missed and retake the exam. Grades are now determined by how much content they have mastered.

How Flipping Works for You

Save time stop repeating you

Record re-usable videos lessons, so you don't have to do it again next year, It's easy to make minor updates to perfect lessons over time once the initial recording is done.

Spend more time with students

Build stronger student teacher relationships and promote higher level thinking. Since your class will watch the lectures as homework, you can spend class time working one on one with students to get them beyond simple memorization.

Let students take control of their learning

Not all students learn at the same pace. Allow students to rewind and replay your lectures. Give students the time they need to process the lesson, so they come to school prepared to ask the questions they need answered.

Flipping the Elementary Classroom

A flipped classroom flips, or reverses, traditional teaching methods. Traditionally, the teacher talks about a topic at school and assigns homework that reinforces that day's material. In a flipped classroom, the instruction is delivered online, outside of class. Video lectures may be online or may be provided on a DVD or a thumb drive. Some flipped models include communicating with classmates and the teacher via online discussions. The recorded lecture can be paused, rewound, re-watched and forwarded through as needed. Then, class time is spent doing what ordinarily may have been assigned as homework. Class time may also be spent doing exercises, projects, discussions, or other interactive activities that illustrate the concept.

At the heart of the flipped classroom model is the desire to have classrooms be more active and engaging, and to give teachers more time to interact directly with students in small group or individual settings. Most flipped classrooms are in high schools and colleges. This makes sense when you consider the amount of lecture that takes place in upper-level classrooms.

4 Benefits of the Flipped Classroom

The idea of the flipped classroom has been sweeping through the education community. The concept isn't complicated, but it is most definitely a departure from traditional teaching. Students learn new material at home using videos or other tools provided by teachers. In class, they focus on what would have traditionally been homework.

Why are schools flipping classrooms?

More efficient for teachers

While there is an initial up-front investment that teachers have to make to set up a flipped classroom – creating a video can take 15 minutes or two days – they can ultimately save a lot of time using this model. In the future, recorded lesson plans and collected resources can be easily transferred to other classes. Plus, if students miss a class, teachers don't have to spend time going over missed material because it's all online.

Students control their learning

Research has shown that we all learn in different ways and at different speeds. If students are learning content at home, they can take their time to read through a passage, re-watch a video lecture or even initiate a Google search to better understand an idea. Instructors can also post multiple kinds of materials so that students are more likely to find a source that will help them, whether it's an article, video or interactive tool.

Inexpensive for schools to implement

Besides investing in a new video cameras or better classroom computers, the only other thing you need is time. This model is much more cost-effective for schools than purchasing hundreds of new classroom gadgets to increase engagement.

Versatile, engaging way to share content

One of the greatest things about this model is that teachers can share so many different kinds of content. Learning isn't restricted to a whiteboard or textbook. Instead, students can be directed to any website, mobile application or other kind of content. Teachers can create learning modules that allow students to quickly jump from one resource to the next.

Benefits of a flipped classroom

Students	Teachers
• Students learn at varying speeds	• Teachers focus on being the 'guide on the side' not the 'sage on the stage'

- Students are provided opportunities for review
- Lessons front-load students for classroom activities
- Materials are ready and prepared for students who are absent or sick
- Parents can view lessons and better assist students
- Students do not struggle with completing home work because they forgot how
- Students take ownership of their learning
- Students are actively working with their peers

- Teachers spend more time supporting students with practice
- Teachers are involved with student learning rather than lecture
- Teachers spend less time on classroom management of student behaviors
- Teachers are able to provide one on one and small group assistance
- Teachers are not spending extra hours tutoring and re explaining to students who did not understand the class lesson
- Teachers collaborate with peers in creating materials
- Teachers connect with students

The Advantages

1. Students are able to approach material and take it in at their own speed
2. By covering lecture material at home and from a video-based platform, students can privately view the material.

3. This allows them to approach things at their own pace without worry of peers noticing them moving slower or faster.
4. Students can stop, pause, rewind, and fast forward material so that they can examine things in their own way.
5. By taking the lecture portion of the classroom home with them, students are able to utilize their teachers' one-on-one attention more successfully in the classroom.
6. Students sit through lecture, gather questions, and prepare themselves for the day with the teacher to tackle "homework".
7. Because the actual exercises are done in the classroom rather than at home with this model, students have their teacher available for questions with problems when they occur.
8. The flipped classroom also allows teaching to adapt more easily to the different teaching styles that individual students may be most successful with.
9. By putting lectures in a video format, students can listen to the lesson and watch the video illustrate the lesson.
10. We want a lecture that explains concepts verbally, but also draws them out in images and pictures.
11. This provides adequate learning opportunities for verbal learners and for visual learners. With in-classroom lecturing, the visual aspect of lecturing can be significantly more difficult to accomplish.

The Disadvantages

1. The flipped classroom method is not going to accommodate every individual perfectly.
2. The biggest setback today to the flipped classroom method is that not all students and schools have access to technologies that can really work for this method.
3. Students from lower income areas and lower income families may not have access to the computers and internet technologies that the flipped classroom requires.

4. The structure really hinges on every student having personal access to his or her own personal device.
5. This simply is not the case for every student and every school district.
6. Students who do not have personal home computers or access to the internet would be forced to use public computers at a library or at the school.
7. Flipped classroom that many people bring up is the fact that students would be spending all of their "homework time" plugged-in in front of a computer screen.
8. Not only do not all students do well with learning from a screen, but this also adds to a student's time in front of a screen and sitting sedentary.
9. While this concern isn't singular to the flipped classroom, the teaching concept doesn't help our young students to get up and get away from their computers, televisions, and iPods.

Conclusion

Flipped classrooms have the opportunity to cause a significant shift in the way instruction is delivered. Using technology, teachers are now able to provide an alternative to traditional lecture-based models by implementing a blended learning method that combines the benefits of direct instruction and active learning to engage students in the learning process

The method itself, while not difficult to initiate, requires a set of technical skills, conceptual knowledge and pedagogical expertise to implement effectively. Delivering those skills through a single module is best accomplished through a broad approach that provides users with an overview of the method and gives them the proper skills and expertise to get started.

To enhance their knowledge, participants must be exposed to working examples within their area of instruction to build confidence in their ability to implement the method on their own. Access to support communities should also be made available to provide guidance and expand on the learned experiences shared by their peers.

References

1. Petress, K. (2008). What Is Meant by "Active Learning? Education, 128(4), 566-569.
2. Seizer, R. (2010). Pulling out All the Stops Education, 130(3), 416-423.
3. Tucker, B. (2012) the Flipped Classroom Education Next, 12 (1). Retrieved from http://educationnext.org/the-flipped-classroom

25

Passive to Active Learning

Introduction

In "flipped classes" students use technology at home to watch online video lectures, demonstrations, and explanations of assignments. Class time is spent doing what is traditionally called "homework." The teacher in a flipped classroom is a learning facilitator, able to work one-to-one with students, clarify assignments, and offer help as needed. Classmates can work together on in-class assignments, engage in discussions, or collaborate on projects. A major benefit is that teachers spend more time working directly with students instead of lecturing to them. The downside is the need for access to technology and the student's own motivation to watch the videos. While often defined simplistically as "school work at home and home work at school," Flipped Learning is an approach that allows teachers to implement a methodology, or various methodologies, in their classrooms.

In terms of Bloom's revised taxonomy (2001), this means that students are doing the lower levels of cognitive work (gaining knowledge and comprehension) outside of class, and focusing on the higher forms of cognitive work (application, analysis, synthesis, and/or evaluation) in class, where they have the support of their peers and instructor. This model contrasts from the traditional model in which "first exposure" occurs via lecture in class, with students assimilating knowledge through homework; thus the term "flipped classroom."

Flip Teaching

Flip teaching or a flipped classroom is a form of blended learning in which students learn new content online by watching video lectures, usually at home, and what used to be homework (assigned problems) is now done in class with teachers offering more personalized guidance and interaction with students, instead of lecturing. This is also known as backwards classroom, flipped classroom, reverse teaching, and the Thayer Method.

What is a 'Flipped Classroom'?

The flipped classroom describes a reversal of traditional teaching where students gain first exposure to new material outside of class, usually via reading or lecture videos, and then class time is used to do the harder work of assimilating that knowledge through strategies such as problem-solving, discussion or debates.

The purpose of flipping the classroom is to shift from passive to active learning to focus on the higher order thinking skills such as analysis, synthesis and evaluation (Bloom). There are many permutations of what a flipped classroom will look like and depends on variables such as class size, resources, support and readiness to change. At UQ, several teachers across the faculties have already flipped their classrooms and their valuable experiences have been captured in the Case Studies section.

In the flipped classroom, the roles and expectations of students and teachers change where:

- Students take more responsibility for their own learning and study core content either individually or in groups before class and then apply knowledge and skills to a range of activities using higher order thinking,

- Teaching 'one-to-many' focuses more on facilitation and moderation than lecturing, though lecturing is still important. Significant learning opportunities can be gained through facilitating active learning, engaging students, guiding learning, correcting misunderstandings and providing timely feedback using a variety of pedagogical strategies,

There is a greater focus on concept exploration, meaning making and demonstration or application of knowledge in the face-to-face setting Educational technologies (see Diagram 2) are an important feature of the flipped classroom as they can be used to:

- **Capture key content** for students to access at their own convenience and to suit their pace of learning (e.g. lecture material, readings, interactive multimedia),
- **Present learning materials** in a variety of formats to suit different learner styles (e.g. text, videos, audio, multimedia),
- **Provide opportunities for discourse** and interaction in and out of class (e.g. polling tools, discussion tools, content creation tools),
- **Convey timely information**, updates and reminders for students (e.g. micro-blogging, announcement tools),
- **Provide immediate and anonymous feedback** for teachers and students (e.g. quizzes, polls) to signal revision points,
- **Capture data** about students to analyze their progress and identify 'at risk' students (e.g. analytics).

Benefits of Flipped Classroom

1. Extend learning beyond normal the school day
2. Increase the quality and quantity of interactions between teacher and student
3. Encourage students to work at their own pace, stopping, rewinding and reviewing lessons as needed
4. Accommodate diverse learning styles by providing instructional materials in a variety of formats

Conclusion

Flipping also changes the allocation of teacher time. Traditionally, the teacher engages with the students who ask questions — but those who don't ask tend to need the most attention. "We refer to 'silent failures,' said one teacher, claiming that flipping allows her to target those who need the most help rather than the most confident. Flipping changes teachers from "sage on the stage" to "guide on the side", allowing them to work with individuals or groups of students.

Of the over 180,000 middle and high school students who participated in the Speak Up 2013 surveys, almost three-quarters of these students agree that flipped learning would be a good way for them to learn, with 32 percent of those students strongly agreeing with that idea.

Bibliography

1. Angelo, T. A., & Cross, K. P. (1993). Classroom Assessment Techniques. San Fransisco: Jossey - Bass.
2. Bergman, J. (2012). Retrieved November 26, 2012, from Flipped Learning - Turning Learning on Its Head: http:// flipped - learning.com

26

Cloud Computing

Introduction

Cloud computing is nothing but a network of all programs and applications on many connected computers at the same time. This may in all fields. They can simply log on to the network without installing anything. Network based services, which appear to be provided by real server hardware and are in fact served up by install hardware. Cloud computing will be used by many resources. The users are dynamically effectively reallocating all these system with cloud computing, multiple users can access a single server to retrieve and update without purchasing licenses for different applications.

It is used for different types of software services. In remote location, cloud computing services are useful. IT has good growth and popularity. It is the result of evolution and adoption of existing technologies and paradigms. In this computing, virtualization generalizes the physical infrastructure, which is east to manage and use. It shares many characteristics with client server model, cloud computing, mainframe computer, utility computer, utility computing, peer-to-peer cloud gaming etc. Its cost reduces. A public – cloud delivery model converts capital expenditure to operational expenditure.

Cloud computing

Cloud computing in general can be portrayed as a synonym for distributed computing over a network, with the ability to run a program or application on many connected computers at the same time. It specifically refers to a computing hardware machine or group of computing hardware machines commonly referred as a server connected through a communication network such as the Internet, an intranet, a local area network (LAN) or wide area network (WAN) and individual users or user who have permission to access the server can use the server's processing power for their individual computing needs like to run a application, store data or any other computing need. Therefore, instead of using a personal computer every-time to run the application, the individual can now run the application from anywhere in the world, as the server provides the processing power to the application and the server is also connected to a network via internet or other connection platforms to be accessed from anywhere [30]. All this has become possible due to increasing computer processing power available to humankind with decrease in cost as stated in Moore's law.

In common usage, the term "the cloud" is essentially a metaphor for the Internet. Marketers have further popularized the phrase "in the cloud" to refer to software, platforms and infrastructure that are sold "as a service", i.e. remotely through the Internet. Typically, the seller has actual energy-consuming servers which host products and services from a remote location, so end-users don't have to; they can simply log on to the network without installing anything. The major models of cloud computing service are known as software as a service, platform as a service, and infrastructure as a service. These cloud services may be offered in a public, private or hybrid network.[2] Google, Amazon,IBM, Oracle Cloud, Rackspace, Salesforce, Zoho and Microsoft Azure are some well-known cloud vendors.

Network-based services, which appear to be provided by real server hardware and are in fact served up by virtual hardware simulated by software running on one or more real machines, is often called cloud computing. Such virtual servers do not physically exist and can therefore be moved around and scaled up or down on the fly without affecting the end user, somewhat like a cloud becoming larger or smaller without being a physical object.

Advantages

Cloud computing relies on sharing of resources to achieve coherence and economies of scale, similar to a utility (like the electricity) over a network. At the foundation of cloud computing is the broader concept of infrastructure and shared services.

The cloud also focuses on maximizing the effectiveness of the shared resources. Cloud resources are usually not only shared by multiple users but are also dynamically reallocated per demand. This can work for allocating resources to users. For example, a cloud computer facility that serves European users during European business hours with a specific application (e.g., email) may reallocate the same resources to serve North American users during North America's business hours with a different application (e.g., a web server). This approach should maximize the use of computing power thus reducing environmental damage as well since less power, air conditioning, rack space, etc. are required for a variety of functions. With cloud computing, multiple users can access a single server to retrieve and update their data without purchasing licenses for different applications.

The term "moving to cloud" also refers to an organization moving away from a traditional CAPEX model (buy the dedicated hardware and depreciate it over a period of time) to the OPEX model (use a shared cloud infrastructure and pay as one uses it).

Proponents claim that cloud computing allows companies to avoid upfront infrastructure costs, and focus on projects that differentiate their businesses instead of infrastructure. Proponents also claim that cloud computing allows enterprises to get their applications up and running faster, with improved manageability and less maintenance, and enables IT to more rapidly adjust resources to meet fluctuating and unpredictable business demand. Cloud providers typically use a “pay as you go” model. This can lead to unexpectedly high charges if administrators do not adapt to the cloud pricing model.

Hosted (Host) services

The term “cloud computing” is mostly used to sell hosted services in the sense of application service provisioning that run client software at a remote location. Such services are given popular acronyms like ‘SaaS’ (Software as a Service), ‘PaaS’ (Platform as a Service), ‘IaaS’ (Infrastructure as a Service), ‘HaaS’ (Hardware as a Service) and finally ‘EaaS’ (Everything as a Service). End users access cloud-based applications through a web browser, thin client or mobile app while the business software and user’s data are stored on servers at a remote location. Examples include Amazon Web Services and Google App engine, which allocate space for a user to deploy and manage software “in the cloud”.

History The 1950s

The underlying concept of computing dates back to the 1950s, when large-scale mainframe computers became available in academia and corporations, accessible via thin clients/terminal computers, often referred to as “static terminals”, because they were used for communications but had no internal processing capacities. To make more efficient use of costly mainframes, a practice evolved that allowed multiple users to share both the physical access to the computer from multiple terminals as well as the CPU time. This eliminated periods of inactivity on the mainframe and allowed for a greater return on the investment. The practice of sharing CPU time on a mainframe became known in the industry as time-sharing. During mid 70s it was popularly known as RJE Remote Job Entry process mostly associated with IBM and DEC.

The 1960s–1990s

John McCarthy opined in the 1960s that “computation may someday be organized as a public utility.” Almost all of the modern-day characteristics of cloud computing (elastic provision, provided as a utility, online, illusion of infinite supply), the comparison to the electricity industry and the use of public, private, government, and community forms, were thoroughly explored in Douglas HYPERLINK "http://en.wikipedia.org/wiki/Douglas_Parkhill"Parkhill's 1966 book, The Challenge of the Computer Utility. Other scholars have shown that cloud computing roots go all the way back to the 1950s when scientist Herb HYPERLINK "http://en.wikipedia.org/wiki/Herb_Grosch"Grosch (the author of Grosch'sHYPERLINK "http://en.wikipedia.org/wiki/Grosch%27s_law" law) postulated that the entire world would operate on dumb terminals powered by about 15 large data centers.[11] Due to the expense of these powerful computers, many corporations and other entities could avail themselves of computing capability through time-sharing and several organizations, such as GE's GEISCO, IBM subsidiary The Service Bureau Corporation (SBC, founded in 1957), Tymshare (founded in 1966), National CSS (founded in 1967 and bought by Dun & Bradstreet in 1979), Dial Data (bought by Tymshare in 1968), and Bolt, HYPERLINK "http://en.wikipedia.org/wiki/Bolt, Beranek and Newman" Beranek HYPERLINK "http://en.wikipedia.org/wiki/Bolt, Beranek and Newman" and Newman (BBN) marketed time-sharing as a commercial venture.

The 1990s

In the 1990s, telecommunications companies, who previously offered primarily dedicated point-to-point data circuits, began offering virtual private network (VPN) services with comparable quality of service, but at a lower cost. By switching traffic as they saw fit to balance server use, they could use overall network bandwidth more effectively. They began to use the cloud symbol to denote the demarcation point between what the providers was responsible for and what users were responsible for. Cloud computing extends this boundary to cover servers as well as the network infrastructure.

As computers became more prevalent, scientists and technologists explored ways to make large-scale computing power available to more users through time-sharing, experimenting with algorithms to provide the optimal use of the infrastructure, platform and applications which prioritized the CPU and efficiency for the end users.

Since 2000]

After the dot-com bubble, Amazon played a key role in the development of cloud computing by modernizing their data centers, which, like most computer networks, were using as little as 10% of their capacity at any one time, just to leave room for occasional spikes. Having found that the new cloud architecture resulted in significant internal efficiency improvements whereby small, fast-moving "two-pizza teams" (teams small enough to feed with two pizzas) could add new features faster and more easily, Amazon initiated a new product development effort to provide cloud computing to external customers, and launched Amazon Web Services (AWS) on a utility computing basis in 2006.

In early 2008, Eucalyptus became the first open-source, AWS API-compatible platform for deploying private clouds. In early 2008, Open Nebula, enhanced in the *RESERVOIR* European Commission-funded project, became the first open-source software for deploying private and hybrid clouds, and for the federation of clouds. In the same year, efforts were focused on providing quality of service guarantees (as required by real-time interactive applications) to cloud-based infrastructures, in the framework of the IRMOS European Commission-funded project, resulting in a real-time cloud environment. By mid-2008, Gartner saw an opportunity for cloud computing "to shape the relationship among consumers of IT services, those who use IT services and those who sell them"[18] and observed that "organizations are switching from company-owned hardware and software assets to per-use service-based models" so that the "projected shift to computing ... will result in dramatic growth in IT products in some areas and significant reductions in other areas.

On March 1, 2011, IBM announced the IBM HYPERLINK "http://en.wikipedia.org/wiki/IBM_cloud_computing"Smart Cloud framework to support Smarter Planet. Among the various components of the Smarter Computing foundation, cloud computing is a critical piece. On June 7, 2012, Oracle announced the Oracle Cloud. While aspects of the Oracle Cloud are still in development, this cloud offering is posed to be the first to provide users with access to an integrated set of IT solutions, including the Applications (SaaS), Platform (PaaS), and Infrastructure (IaaS) layers.

Growth and popularity

The development of the Internet from being document centric via semantic data towards more and more services was described as "dynamic web". This contribution focused in particular in the need for better meta-data able to describe not only implementation details but also conceptual details of model-based applications.

The present availability of high-capacity networks, low-cost computers and storage devices as well as the widespread adoption of hardware virtualization, service-oriented architecture, and autonomic and utility computing have led to a growth in cloud computing.

Financials

Cloud vendors are experiencing growth rates of 91% per annum.

Origin of the term

The origin of the term cloud computing is unclear, although it is often attributed to the Internet Systems Division of Compaq Computer (George Favaloro, Philip Reagan, Jeff Whatcott, Ken Evans, Ricardo Cidale, and others). The expression cloud is commonly used in science to describe a large agglomeration of objects that visually appear from a distance as a cloud and describes any set of things whose details are not inspected further in a given context.

5. Meteorology: a weather cloud is an agglomeration.
6. Mathematics: a large number of points in a coordinate system in mathematics is seen as a point cloud;
7. Astronomy: a cloud of gas and particulate matter in space is known as a nebula (Latin for mist or cloud),
8. Physics: The indeterminate position of electrons around an atomic kernel appears like a cloud to a distant observer

In analogy to above usage the word cloud was used as a metaphor for the Internet and a standardized cloud-like shape was used to denote a network on telephony schematics and later to depict the Internet in computer network diagrams. The cloud symbol was used to represent the Internet as early as 1994, in which servers were then shown connected to, but external to, the cloud.

References to cloud computing in its modern sense can be found as early as 1996, with the earliest known mention to be found in a Compaq internal document. The term became popular after Amazon.com introduced the Elastic Compute Cloud in 2006.

Similar systems and concepts

Cloud Computing is the result of evolution and adoption of existing technologies and paradigms. The goal of cloud computing is to allow users to take beneath from all of these technologies, without the need for deep knowledge about or expertise with each one of them. The cloud aims to cut costs, and help the users focus on their core business instead of being impeded by IT obstacles.

The main enabling technology for cloud computing is virtualization. Virtualization generalizes the physical infrastructure, which is the most rigid component, and makes it available as a soft component that is easy to use and manage. By doing so, virtualization provides the agility required to speed up IT operations, and reduces cost by increasing infrastructure utilization. On the other hand, autonomic computing automates the process through which the user can provision resources on-demand. By minimizing user involvement, automation speeds up the process and reduces the possibility of human errors.[34]

Users face difficult business problems every day. Cloud computing adopts concepts from Service-oriented HYPERLINK "http://en.wikipedia.org/wiki/Service-oriented Architecture" Architecture (SOA) that can help the user break these problems into services that can be integrated to provide a solution. Cloud computing provides all of its resources as services, and makes use of the well-established standards and best practices gained in the domain of SOA to allow global and easy access to cloud services in a standardized way.

Cloud computing also leverages concepts from utility computing in order to provide metrics for the services used. Such metrics are at the core of the public cloud pay-per-use models. In addition, measured services are an essential part of the feedback loops in autonomic computing, allowing services to scale on-demand and to perform automatic failure recovery.

Cloud computing is a kind of grid computing; it has evolved by addressing the QoS (quality of service) and reliability problems. Cloud computing provides the tools and technologies to build data/compute intensive parallel applications with much more affordable prices compared to traditional parallel computing techniques. Cloud computing shares characteristics with:

1. Client–server model — Client–server computing refers broadly to any distributed application that distinguishes between service providers (servers) and service requestors (clients).
2. Grid computing — "A form of distributed and parallel computing, whereby a 'super and virtual computer' is composed of a cluster of networked, loosely coupled computers acting in concert to perform very large tasks."
3. Mainframe computer — Powerful computers used mainly by large organizations for critical applications, typically bulk data processing such as: census; industry and consumer statistics; police and secret intelligence services; enterprise resource planning; and financial transaction processing.
4. Utility computing — The "packaging of computing resources, such as computation and storage, as a metered service similar to a traditional public utility, such as electricity."
5. Peer-to-peer — A distributed architecture without the need for central coordination. Participants are both suppliers and consumers of resources (in contrast to the traditional client–server model).
6. Cloud gaming — Also known as on-demand gaming, is a way of delivering games to computers. Gaming data is stored in the provider's server, so that gaming is independent of client computers used to play the game. One such current example, would be a service by On Live which allows users a certain space to save game data, and load games within the On Live server.

Characteristics

Cloud computing exhibits the following key characteristics:

7. Agility improves with users' ability to re-provision technological infrastructure resources.
8. Application programming interface (API) accessibility to software that enables machines to interact with cloud software in the same way that a traditional user interface (e.g., a computer desktop) facilitates interaction between humans and computers. Cloud computing systems typically use Representational State Transfer (REST)-based APIs.
9. Cost: cloud providers claim that computing costs reduce. A public-cloud delivery model converts capital expenditure to operational. This purportedly lowers barriers to entry, as infrastructure is typically provided by a third party and does not need to be purchased for one-time or infrequent intensive computing tasks. Pricing on a utility computing basis is fine-grained, with usage-based options and fewer IT skills are required for implementation (in-house). The e-FISCAL project's state-of-the-art repository contains several articles looking into cost aspects in more detail, most of them concluding that costs savings depend on the type of activities supported and the type of infrastructure available in-house.
10. Device and location Device independence" enable users to access systems using a web browser regardless of their location or what device they use (e.g., PC, mobile phone). As infrastructure is off-site (typically provided by a third-party) and accessed via the Internet, users can connect from anywhere.
11. Virtualization technology allows sharing of servers and storage devices and increased utilization. Applications can be easily migrated from one physical server to another.
12. Multi-tenancy enables sharing of resources and costs across a large pool of users thus allowing for:
13. Centralization of infrastructure in locations with lower costs (such as real estate, electricity, etc.)

14. peak-load capacity increases (users need not engineer for highest possible load-levels)
15. Utilization and efficiency improvements for systems that are often only 10–20% utilized.
16. Reliability improves with the use of multiple redundant sites, which makes well-designed cloud computing suitable for business and disaster recovery.
17. Scalability and elasticity via dynamic ("on-demand") provisioning of resources on a fine-grained, self-service basis in near real-time (Note, the VM startup time varies by VM type, location, os and cloud providers), without users having to engineer for peak loads.
18. Performance is monitored and consistent and loosely coupled architectures are constructed using web services as the system interface.
19. Security can improve due to centralization of data, increased security-focused resources, etc., but concerns can persist about loss of control over certain sensitive data, and the lack of security for stored kernels. Security is often as good as or better than other traditional systems, in part because providers are able to devote resources to solving security issues that many customers cannot afford to tackle. However, the complexity of security is greatly increased when data is distributed over a wider area or over a greater number of devices, as well as in multi-tenant systems shared by unrelated users. In addition, user access to security audit logs may be difficult or impossible. Private cloud installations are in part motivated by users' desire to retain control over the infrastructure and avoid losing control of information security.
20. Maintenance of cloud computing applications is easier, because they do not need to be installed on each user's computer and can be accessed from different places.

The National Institute of Standards and Technology's definition of cloud computing identifies "five essential characteristics":

On-demand self-service: A consumer can unilaterally provision computing capabilities, such as server time and network storage, as needed automatically without requiring human interaction with each service provider.

Broad network access: Capabilities are available over the network and accessed through standard mechanisms that promote use by heterogeneous thin or thick client platforms (e.g., mobile phones, tablets, laptops, and workstations).

Resource pooling: The provider's computing resources are pooled to serve multiple consumers using a multi-tenant model, with different physical and virtual resources dynamically assigned and reassigned according to consumer demand.

Rapid elasticity: Capabilities can be elastically provisioned and released, in some cases automatically, to scale rapidly outward and inward commensurate with demand. To the consumer, the capabilities available for provisioning often appear unlimited and can be appropriated in any quantity at any time.

Measured service: Cloud systems automatically control and optimize resource use by leveraging a metering capability at some level of abstraction appropriate to the type of service (e.g., storage, processing, bandwidth, and active user accounts). Resource usage can be monitored, controlled, and reported, providing transparency for both the provider and consumer of the utilized service-National Institute of Standards and Technology.

On-demand self-service

On-demand self-service allows users to obtain, configure and deploy cloud services themselves using cloud service catalogues, without requiring the assistance of IT. This feature is listed by the National Institute of Standards and Technology (NIST) as a characteristic of cloud computing.

The self-service requirement of cloud computing prompts infrastructure vendors to create cloud computing templates, which are obtained from cloud service catalogues. Manufacturers of such templates or blueprints include BMC Software (BMC), with Service

Blueprints as part of their cloud management platform Hewlett-Packard (HP), which names its templates as HP Cloud Maps, Right Scale and Red Hat, which names its templates Cloud forms.

The templates contain predefined configurations used by consumers to set up cloud services. The templates or blueprints provide the technical information necessary to build ready-to-use clouds. Each template includes specific configuration details for different cloud infrastructures, with information about servers for specific tasks such as hosting applications, databases, websites and so on. The templates also include predefined Web service, the operating system, the database, security configurations and load balancing.

Cloud computing consumers use cloud templates to move applications between clouds through a self-service portal. The predefined blueprints define all that an application requires to run in different environments. For example, a template could define how the same application could be deployed in cloud platforms based on Amazon Web Services, VMware or Red Hat. The user organization benefits from cloud templates because the technical aspects of cloud configurations reside in the templates, letting users deploy cloud services with a push of a button. Developers can use cloud templates to create a catalog of cloud services.

Service models

Cloud computing providers offer their services according to several fundamental models: infrastructure as a service (IaaS), platform as a service (PaaS), and software as a service (SaaS) where IaaS is the most basic and each higher model abstracts from the details of the lower models. Other key components in anything as a service (XaaS) are described in a comprehensive taxonomy model published in 2009, such as Strategy-as-a-Service, Collaboration-as-a-Service, Business Process-as-a-Service, Database-as-a-Service, etc. In 2012, network as a service (NaaS) and communication as a service (CaaS) were officially included by ITU (International Telecommunication Union) as part of the basic cloud computing models, recognized service categories of a telecommunication-centric cloud ecosystem.

Infrastructure as a service

In the most basic cloud-service model, providers of IaaS offer computers – physical or (more often) virtual machines-and other resources. (A hypervisor, such as OpenStack, Xen, KVM, VMware ESX/HYPERLINK "http://en.wikipedia.org/wiki/VMware_ESX"ESXi, or Hyper-V runs the virtual machines as guests. Pools of hypervisors within the cloud operational support-system can support large numbers of virtual machines and the ability to scale services up and down according to customers' varying requirements.) IaaS clouds often offer additional resources such as a virtual-machine disk image library, raw (block) and file-based storage, firewalls, load balancers, IP addresses, virtual local area networks (VLANs), and software bundles. IaaS-cloud providers supply these resources on-demand from their large pools installed in data centers. For wide-area connectivity, customers can use either the Internet or carrier clouds (dedicated virtual private networks).

To deploy their applications, cloud users install operating-system images and their application software on the cloud infrastructure. In this model, the cloud user patches and maintains the operating systems and the application software. Cloud providers typically bill IaaS services on a utility computing basis: cost reflects the amount of resources allocated and consumed.

Cloud communications and cloud telephony, rather than replacing local computing infrastructure, replace local telecommunications infrastructure with Voice over IP and other off-site Internet services.

Platform as a service

In the PaaS models, cloud providers deliver a computing platform, typically including operating system, programming language execution environment, database, and web server. Application developers can develop and run their software solutions on a cloud platform without the cost and complexity of buying and managing the underlying hardware and software layers. With some PaaS offers like Windows Azure, the underlying computer and storage resources scale automatically to match application demand so that the cloud user does not have to allocate resources manually. The latter has also been proposed by an architecture aiming to facilitate real-time in cloud environments.

Software as a service

In the business model using software as a service (SaaS), users are provided access to application software and databases. Cloud providers manage the infrastructure and platforms that run the applications. SaaS is sometimes referred to as "on-demand software" and is usually priced on a pay-per-use basis. SaaS providers generally price applications using a subscription fee.

In the SaaS model, cloud providers install and operate application software in the cloud and cloud users access the software from cloud clients. Cloud users do not manage the cloud infrastructure and platform where the application runs. This eliminates the need to install and run the application on the cloud user's own computers, which simplifies maintenance and support. Cloud applications are different from other applications in their scalability—which can be achieved by cloning tasks onto multiple virtual machines at run-time to meet changing work demand. Load balancers distribute the work over the set of virtual machines. This process is transparent to the cloud user, who sees only a single access point. To accommodate a large number of cloud users, cloud applications can be multitenant, that is, any machine serves more than one cloud user organization. It is common to refer to special types of cloud-based application software with a similar naming convention: desktop as a service, business process as a service, test environment as a service, communication as a service.

The pricing model for SaaS applications is typically a monthly or yearly flat fee per user, so price is scalable and adjustable if users are added or removed at any point. Proponents claim SaaS allows a business the potential to reduce IT operational costs by outsourcing hardware and software maintenance and support to the cloud provider. This enables the business to reallocate IT operations costs away from hardware/software spending and personnel expenses, towards meeting other goals. In addition, with applications hosted centrally, updates can be released without the need for users to install new software. One drawback of SaaS is that the users' data are stored on the cloud provider's server. As a result, there could be unauthorized access to the data. For this reason, users are increasingly adopting intelligent third-party key management systems to help secure their data.

Security as a service

Security as a service (SECaaS) is a business model in which a large service provider integrates their security services into a corporate infrastructure on a subscription basis more cost effectively than most individuals or corporations can provide on their own, when total cost of ownership is considered. These security services often include authentication, anti-virus, anti-malware/spyware, intrusion detection, and security event management, among others Cloud management

Legacy management infrastructures, which are based on the concept of dedicated system relationships and architecture constructs, are not well suited to cloud environments where instances are continually launched and decommissioned. Instead, the dynamic nature of cloud computing requires monitoring and management tools that are adaptable, extensible and customizable.

Cloud management challenges

Cloud computing presents a number of management challenges. Companies using public clouds do not have ownership of the equipment hosting the cloud environment, and because the environment is not contained within their own networks, public cloud customers do not have full visibility or control. Users of public cloud services must also integrate with an architecture defined by the cloud provider, using its specific parameters for working with cloud components. Integration includes tying into the cloud APIs for configuring IP addresses, subnets, firewalls and data service functions for storage. Because control of these functions is based on the cloud provider's infrastructure and services, public cloud users must integrate with the cloud infrastructure management.

Capacity management is a challenge for both public and private cloud environments because end users have the ability to deploy applications using self-service portals. Applications of all sizes may appear in the environment, consume an unpredictable amount of resources and then disappear at any time.

Chargeback—or, pricing resource use on a granular basis—is a challenge for both public and private cloud environments. Chargeback is a challenge for public cloud service providers because they must price their services competitively while still creating profit. Users of public cloud services may find chargeback challenging because it is difficult for IT groups to assess actual resource costs on a granular basis due to overlapping resources within an organization that may be paid for by an individual business unit, such as electrical power. For private cloud operators, chargeback is fairly straightforward, but the challenge lies in guessing how to allocate resources as closely as possible to actual resource usage to achieve the greatest operational efficiency. Exceeding budgets can be a risk.

Hybrid cloud environments, which combine public and private cloud services, sometimes with traditional infrastructure elements, present their own set of management challenges. These include security concerns if sensitive data lands on public cloud servers, budget concerns around overuse of storage or bandwidth and proliferation of mismanaged images. Managing the information flow in a hybrid cloud environment is also a significant challenge. On-premises clouds must share information with applications hosted off-premises by public cloud providers and this information may change constantly. Hybrid cloud environments also typically include a complex mix of policies, permissions and limits that must be managed consistently across both public and private clouds.

Cloud clients

Users access cloud computing using networked client devices, such as desktop computers, laptops, tablets and smart phones. Some of these devices – cloud clients – rely on cloud computing for all or a majority of their applications so as to be essentially useless without it. Examples are thin clients and the browser-based Chrome book. Many cloud applications do not require specific software on the client and instead use a web browser to interact with the cloud application. With Ajax and HTML5 these Web user interfaces can achieve a similar, or even better, look and feel to native applications. Some cloud applications, however, support specific client software dedicated to these applications (e.g., virtual desktop clients and most email clients). Some legacy applications (line of business applications that until now have been prevalent in thin client computing) are delivered via a screen-sharing technology.

Deployment models

Controlled cloud services are not publicly available; users are specifically authorized by services vendors. Access to the controlled cloud may be through the Internet; however, connections would be encrypted. The cloud vendor employs various techniques and technologies to prevent unauthorized access. Use of services is governed by contracts, and which specify the responsibilities of the vendor and the responsibilities of the customer with regard to data stewardship.

The services vendor discloses to customers its processes for managing customer data. Any sub processors used in processing customer data are identified to customers. Data protection schemes, such as administrative controls, encryption methods, and other appropriate technical and organizational measures (TOMs) to protect data are described and demonstrated to customers.

The services vendor undergoes audits by an accredited independent third party using an industry standard such as the Service Organization Controls" Organization Controls as defined by the AICPA, or achieves certification of an industry standard such as the Internationa Standards Organization (ISO) 27001:2005 for information security or the British Standard BS 10012 for data privacy. Services vendors and their sub processors provide customers with the ability to view or receive copies of audit reports and certifications relevant to their cloud offerings and will actively inform their customers (users) about any security breach and data leakage or misuse.

Private cloud

Private cloud is cloud infrastructure operated solely for a single organization, whether managed internally or by a third-party and hosted internally or externally. Undertaking a private cloud project requires a significant level and degree of engagement to virtualize the business environment, and requires the organization to reevaluate decisions about existing resources. When done right, it can improve business, but every step in the project raises security issues that must be addressed to prevent serious vulnerabilities.[84] Self-run data centers are generally capital intensive. They have a significant physical footprint, requiring allocations of space, hardware, and environmental controls. These assets have to be refreshed periodically, resulting in additional capital expenditures. They have attracted criticism because users "still have to buy, build, and manage them" and thus do not benefit from less hands-on management, essentially "[lacking] the economic model that makes cloud computing such an intriguing concept."

Public cloud

A cloud is called a "public cloud" when the services are rendered over a network that is open for public use. Technically there may be little or no difference between public and private cloud architecture, however, security consideration may be substantially different for services (applications, storage, and other resources) that are made available by a service provider for a public audience and when communication is effected over a non-trusted network. Generally, public cloud service providers like Amazon AWS, Microsoft and Google own and operate the infrastructure and offer access only via Internet.

Community cloud

Community cloud shares infrastructure between several organizations from a specific community with common concerns (security, compliance, jurisdiction, etc.), whether managed internally or by a third-party and hosted internally or externally. The costs are spread over fewer users than a public cloud (but more than a private cloud), so only some of the cost savings potential of cloud computing are realized.

Hybrid cloud

Hybrid cloud is a composition of two or more clouds (private, community or public) that remain distinct entities but are bound together, offering the benefits of multiple deployment models. Hybrid cloud can also mean the ability to connect collocation, managed and/ or dedicated services with cloud resources.

Gartner, Inc. defines a hybrid cloud service as a cloud computing service that is composed of some combination of private, public and community cloud services, from different service providers. A hybrid cloud service crosses isolation and provider boundaries so that it can't be simply put in one category of private, public, or community cloud service. It allows one to extend either the capacity or the capability of a cloud service, by aggregation, integration or customization with another cloud service.

Varied use cases for hybrid cloud composition exist. For example, an organization may store sensitive client data in house on a private cloud application, but interconnect that application to a billing application provided on a public cloud as a software service. This example of hybrid cloud extends the capabilities of the enterprise to deliver a specific business service through the addition of externally available public cloud services.

Another example of hybrid cloud is one where IT organizations use public cloud computing resources to meet temporary capacity needs that cannot be met by the private cloud. This capability enables hybrid clouds to employ cloud bursting for scaling across clouds.

Cloud bursting is an application deployment model in which an application runs in a private cloud or data center and "bursts" to a public cloud when the demand for computing capacity increases. A primary advantage of cloud bursting and a hybrid cloud model is that an organization only pays for extra compute resources when they are needed.

Cloud bursting enables data centers to create an in-house IT infrastructure that supports average workloads, and use cloud resources from public or private clouds, during spikes in processing demands.

By utilizing "hybrid cloud" architecture, companies and individuals are able to obtain degrees of fault tolerance combined with locally immediate usability without dependency on internet connectivity. Hybrid cloud architecture requires both on-premises resources and off-site (remote) server-based cloud infrastructure.

Cloud management strategies

Public clouds are managed by public cloud service providers, which include the public cloud environment's servers, storage, networking and data center operations. Users of public cloud services can generally select from three basic categories:

1. User self-provisioning: Customers purchase cloud services directly from the provider, typically through a web form or console interface. The customer pays on a per-transaction basis.
2. Advance provisioning: Customers contract in advance a predetermined amount of resources, which are prepared in advance of service. The customer pays a flat fee or a monthly fee.
3. Dynamic provisioning: The provider allocates resources when the customer needs them, then decommissions them when they are no longer needed. The customer is charged on a pay-per-use basis.

Managing a private cloud requires software tools to help create a virtualized pool of compute resources, provide a self-service portal for end users and handle security, resource allocation, tracking and billing. Management tools for private clouds tend to be service driven, as opposed to resource driven, because cloud environments are typically highly virtualized and organized in terms of portable workloads.

In hybrid cloud environments, compute, network and storage resources must be managed across multiple domains, so a good management strategy should start by defining what needs to be managed, and where and how to do it. Policies to help govern these domains should include configuration and installation of images, access control, and budgeting and reporting. Access control often includes the use of Single sign-on (SSO), in which a user logs in once and gains access to all systems without being prompted to log in again at each of them.

Aspects of cloud management systems

A cloud management system is a combination of software and technologies designed to manage cloud environments. The industry has responded to the management challenges of cloud computing with cloud management systems. HP, Novell, Eucalyptus, Open Nebula, Citrix and are among the vendors that have management systems specifically for managing cloud environments.

At a minimum, a cloud management solution should be able to manage a pool of heterogeneous compute resources, provide access to end users, monitor security, manage resource allocation and manage tracking. For composite applications, cloud management solutions also encompass frameworks for workflow mapping and management.

Enterprises with large-scale cloud implementations may require more robust cloud management tools that include specific characteristics, such as the ability to manage multiple platforms from a single point of reference, include intelligent analytics to automate processes like application lifecycle management. And high-end cloud management tools should also be able to handle system failures automatically with capabilities such as self-monitoring, an explicit notification mechanism, and include failover and self-healing capabilities. Cisco recently launched its Inter Cloud solution to provide flexibility to dynamically manage workloads across public and private cloud environments.

Architecture

Cloud architecture, the systems architecture of the software systems involved in the delivery of cloud computing, typically involves multiple cloud components communicating with each other over a loose coupling mechanism such as a messaging queue. Elastic provision implies intelligence in the use of tight or loose coupling as applied to mechanisms such as these and others.

Cloud engineering

Cloud engineering is the application of engineering disciplines to cloud computing. It brings a systematic approach to the high-level concerns of commercialization, standardization, and governance in conceiving, developing, operating and maintaining cloud computing systems. It is a multidisciplinary method encompassing contributions from diverse areas such as systems, software, web, performance, nformation, security, platform, risk, and quality engineering.

Threats and opportunities of the cloud

Critical voices including GNU project initiator Richard Stallman and Oracle founder Larry Ellison warned that the whole concept is rife with privacy and ownership concerns and constitute merely a fad.

However, cloud computing continues to gain steam with 56% of the major European technology decision-makers estimate that the cloud is a priority in 2013 and 2014, and the cloud budget may reach 30% of the overall IT budget. According to the Tec nights Report 2013: Cloud Succeeds based on a survey, the cloud implementations generally meets or exceeds expectations across major service models, such as Infrastructure as a Service (IaaS), Platform as a Service (PaaS) and Software as a Service.

Several deterrents to the widespread adoption of cloud computing remain. Among them, are: reliability, availability of services and data, security, complexity, costs, regulations and legal issues, performance, migration, reversion, the lack of standards, limited customization and issues of privacy. The cloud offers many strong points: infrastructure flexibility, faster deployment of applications and data, cost control, adaptation of cloud resources to real needs, improved productivity, etc. The early 2010s cloud market is dominated by software and services in SaaS mode and IaaS (infrastructure), especially the private cloud. PaaS and the public cloud are further back.

Privacy

The increased use of cloud computing services such as Gmail and Google Docs has pressed the issue of privacy concerns of cloud computing services to the utmost importance.[109] The provider of such services lie in a position such that with the greater use of cloud computing services has given access to a plethora of data. This access has the immense risk of data being disclosed either accidentally or deliberately. Privacy advocates have criticized the cloud model for giving hosting companies' greater ease to control—and thus, to monitor at will—communication between host company and end user, and access user data (with or without permission). Instances such as the secret NSA program, working with AT&T, and Verizon, which recorded over 10 million telephone calls between American citizens, causes uncertainty among privacy advocates, and the greater powers it gives to telecommunication companies to monitor user activity. A cloud service provider (CSP) can complicate data privacy because of the extent of virtualization (virtual machines) and cloud storage used to implement cloud service. CSP operations, customer or tenant data may not remain on the same system, or in the same data center or even within the same provider's cloud; this can lead to legal concerns over jurisdiction. While there have been efforts (such as US-EU Safe Harbor) to "harmonise" the legal environment, providers such as Amazon still cater to major markets (typically to the United States and the European Union) by deploying local infrastructure and allowing customers to select "regions and availability zones". Cloud computing poses privacy concerns because the service provider can access the data that is on the cloud at any time. It could accidentally or deliberately alter or even delete information. This becomes a major concern as these service providers, who employ administrators which can leave room for potential unwanted disclosure of information on the cloud.

Privacy solutions

Solutions to privacy in cloud computing include policy and legislation as well as end users' choices for how data is stored. The cloud service provider needs to establish clear and relevant policies that describe how the data of each cloud user will be accessed and used. Cloud service users can encrypt data that is processed or stored within the cloud to prevent unauthorized access.

Compliance

To comply with regulations including FISMA, HIPAA, and SOX in the United States, the Data Protection Directive in the EU and the credit card industry's PCI DSS, users may have to adopt community or hybrid deployment modes that are typically more expensive and may offer restricted benefits. This is how Google is able to "manage and meet additional government policy requirements beyond FISMA" and Rack space Cloud or QubeSpace are able to claim PCI compliance.

Many providers also obtain a SAS 70 Type II audit, but this has been criticized on the grounds that the hand-picked set of goals and standards determined by the auditor and the audile are often not disclosed and can vary widely. Providers typically make this information available on request, under non-disclosure agreement.

U.S. Federal Agencies have been directed by the Office of Management and Budget to use a process called FedRAMP (Federal Risk and Authorization Management Program) to assess and authorize cloud products and services. Federal CIO Steven VanRoekel issued a memorandum to federal agency Chief Information Officers on December 8, 2011 defining how federal agencies should use FedRAMP. FedRAMP consists of a subset of NIST Special Publication 800-53 security controls specifically selected to provide protection in cloud environments. A subset has been defined for the FIPS 199 low categorization and the FIPS 199 moderate categorization. The FedRAMP program has also established a Joint Accreditation Board (JAB) consisting of Chief Information Officers from DoD, DHS and GSA. The JAB is responsible for establishing accreditation standards for 3rd party organizations that perform the assessments of cloud solutions. The JAB also reviews authorization packages, and may grant provisional authorization (to operate). The federal agency consuming the service still has final responsibility for final authority to operate.

A multitude of laws and regulations have forced specific compliance requirements onto many companies that collect, generate or store data. These policies may dictate a wide array of data storage policies, such as how long information must be retained, the process used for deleting data, and even certain recovery plans. Below are some examples of compliance laws or regulations.

1. United States, the Health Insurance Portability and Accountability Act (HIPAA) requires a contingency plan that includes, data backups, data recovery, and data access during emergencies.
2. The privacy laws of Switzerland demand that private data, including emails, be physically stored in the Switzerland.
3. In the United Kingdom, the Civil Contingencies Act of 2004 sets forth guidance for a Business contingency plan that includes policies for data storage.

In a virtualized cloud computing environment, customers may never know exactly where their data is stored. In fact, data may be stored across multiple data centers in an effort to improve reliability, increase performance, and provide redundancies. This geographic dispersion may make it more difficult to ascertain legal jurisdiction if disputes arise.

Legal

As with other changes in the landscape of computing, certain legal issues arise with cloud computing, including trademark infringement, security concerns and sharing of proprietary data resources. The Electronic Frontier Foundation has criticized the United States government during the Megaupload seizure process for considering that people lose property rights by storing data on a cloud computing service.

One important but not often mentioned problem with cloud computing is the problem of who is in "possession" of the data. If a cloud company is the possessor of the data, the possessor has certain legal rights. If the cloud company is the "custodian" of the data, then a different set of rights would apply. The next problem in the legalities of cloud computing is the problem of legal ownership of the data. Many Terms of Service agreements are silent on the question of ownership.

These legal issues are not confined to the time period in which the cloud-based application is actively being used. There must also be consideration for what happens when the provider-customer relationship ends. In most cases, this event will be addressed before an application is deployed to the cloud. However, in the case of provider insolvencies or bankruptcy the state of the data may become blurred.

Vendor lock-in

Because cloud computing is still relatively new, standards are still being developed. Many cloud platforms and services are proprietary, meaning that they are built on the specific standards, tools and protocols developed by a particular vendor for its particular cloud offering. This can make migrating off a proprietary cloud platform prohibitively complicated and expensive.

Three types of vendor lock-in can occur with cloud computing:

1. Platform lock-in: cloud services tend to be built on one of several possible virtualization platforms, for example VMWare or Xen. Migrating from a cloud provider using one platform to a cloud provider using a different platform could be very complicated.
2. Data lock-in: since the cloud is still new, standards of ownership, i.e. who actually owns the data once it lives on a cloud platform, are not yet developed, which could make it complicated if cloud computing users ever decide to move data off of a cloud vendor's platform.
3. Tools lock-in: if tools built to manage a cloud environment are not compatible with different kinds of both virtual and physical infrastructure, those tools will only be able to manage data or apps that live in the vendor's particular cloud environment.

Heterogeneous cloud computing is described as a type of cloud environment that prevents vendor lock-in, and aligns with enterprise data centers that are operating hybrid cloud models. The absence of vendor lock-in lets cloud administrators select his or her choice of hypervisors for specific tasks, or to deploy virtualized infrastructures to other enterprises without the need to consider the flavor of hypervisor in the other enterprise.

A heterogeneous cloud is considered one that includes on-premise private clouds, public clouds and software-as-a-service clouds. Heterogeneous clouds can work with environments that are not virtualized, such as traditional data centers. Heterogeneous clouds also allow for the use of piece parts, such as hypervisors, servers, and storage, from multiple vendors.

Cloud piece parts, such as cloud storage systems, offer APIs but they are often incompatible with each other. The result is complicated migration between backends, and makes it difficult to integrate data spread across various locations. This has been described as a problem of vendor lock-in. The solution to this is for clouds to adopt common standards.[132]

Heterogeneous cloud computing differs from homogeneous clouds, which have been described as those using consistent building blocks supplied by a single vendor. Intel General Manager of high-density computing, Jason Waxman, is quoted as saying that a homogeneous system of 15,000 servers would cost $6 million more in capital expenditure and use 1 megawatt of power.

Open source

Open-source software has provided the foundation for many cloud computing implementations, prominent examples being the Hadoop framework and VMware's Cloud Foundry.In November 2007, the Free Software Foundation released the Affero General_Public License" General Public License, a version of GPLv3 intended to close a perceived legal loophole associated with free software designed to run over a network.

Open standards

Most cloud providers expose APIs that are typically well documented (often under a Creative Commons license) but also unique to their implementation and thus not interoperable. Some vendors have adopted others' APIs and there are a number of open standards under development, with a view to delivering interoperability and portability. As of November 2012, the Open Standard with broadest industry support is probably OpenStack, founded in 2010 by NASA and Rackspace, and now governed by the OpenStack Foundation. Open Stack supporters include AMD, Intel, Canonical, SUSE Linux, Red Hat, Cisco, Dell, HP, IBM, Yahoo and now VMware.

Security

As cloud computing is achieving increased popularity, concerns are being voiced about the security issues introduced through adoption of this new model. The effectiveness and efficiency of traditional protection mechanisms are being reconsidered as the characteristics of this innovative deployment model can differ widely from those of traditional architectures. An alternative perspective on the topic of cloud security is that this is but another, although quite broad, case of "applied security" and that similar security principles that apply in shared multi-user mainframe security models apply with cloud security.

The relative security of cloud computing services is a contentious issue that may be delaying its adoption. Physical control of the Private Cloud equipment is more secure than having the equipment off site and under someone else's control. Physical control and the ability to visually inspect data links and access ports is required in order to ensure data links are not compromised. Issues barring the adoption of cloud computing are due in large part to the private and public sectors' unease surrounding the external management of security-based services. It is the very nature of cloud computing-based services, private or public, that promote external management of provided services. This delivers great incentive to cloud computing service providers to prioritize building and maintaining strong management of secure services. Security issues have been categorized into sensitive data access, data segregation, privacy, bug exploitation, recovery, accountability, malicious insiders, management console security, account control, and multi-tenancy issues. Solutions to various cloud security issues vary, from cryptography, particularly public key infrastructure (PKI), to use of multiple cloud providers, standardization of APIs, and improving virtual machine support and legal support.

Cloud computing offers many benefits, but is vulnerable to threats. As cloud computing uses increase, it is likely that more criminals find new ways to exploit system vulnerabilities. Many underlying challenges and risks in cloud computing increase the threat of data compromise. To mitigate the threat, cloud computing stakeholders should invest heavily in risk assessment to ensure that the system encrypts to protect data, establishes trusted foundation to secure the platform and infrastructure, and builds higher assurance into auditing to strengthen compliance. Security concerns must be addressed to maintain trust in cloud computing technology.

Data breach is a big concern in cloud computing. A compromised server could significantly harm the users as well as cloud providers. A variety of information could be stolen. These include credit card and social security numbers, addresses, and personal messages. The U.S. now requires cloud providers to notify customers of breaches. Once notified, customers now have to worry about identify theft and fraud. While providers, have to deal with federal investigations, lawsuits, and bad reputation. Customer lawsuits and settlements have resulted in over $1 billion in losses to cloud providers.

Sustainability

Although cloud computing is often assumed to be a form of green computing, there is currently no way to measure how "green" computers are.

The primary environmental problem associated with the cloud is energy use. Phil Radford of Greenpeace said "we are concerned that this new explosion in electricity use could lock us into old, polluting energy sources instead of the clean energy available today." Greenpeace ranks the energy usage of the top ten big brands in cloud computing, and successfully urged several companies to switch to clean energy. On Thursday, December 15, 2011, Greenpeace and Face book announced together that Face book would shift to use clean and renewable energy to power its own operations. Soon thereafter, Apple agreed to make all of its data centers 'coal free' by the end of 2013 and doubled the amount of solar energy powering its Maiden, NC data center. Following suit, Sales force agreed to shift to 100% clean energy by 2020.

Citing the servers' effects on the environmental effects of cloud computing, in areas where climate favors natural cooling and renewable electricity is readily available, the environmental effects will be more moderate. (The same holds true for "traditional" data centers.) Thus countries with favorable conditions, such as Finland, Sweden and Switzerland, are trying to attract cloud computing data centers. Energy efficiency in cloud computing can result from energy-aware scheduling and server consolidation. However, in the case of distributed clouds over data centers with different sources of energy including renewable energy, the use of energy efficiency reduction could result in a significant carbon footprint reduction.

Abuse

As with privately purchased hardware, customers can purchase the services of cloud computing for nefarious purposes. This includes password cracking and launching attacks using the purchased services. In 2009, a banking trojan illegally used the popular Amazon service as a command and control channel that issued software updates and malicious instructions to PCs that were infected by the malware.

IT governance

Corporate governance of information technology the introduction of cloud computing requires an appropriate IT governance model to ensure a secured computing environment and to comply with all relevant organizational information technology policies. As such, organizations need a set of capabilities that are essential when effectively implementing and managing cloud services, including demand management, relationship management, data security management, application lifecycle management; risk and compliance management. A danger lies with the explosion of companies joining the growth in cloud computing by becoming providers. However, many of the infrastructural and logistical concerns regarding the operation of cloud computing businesses are still unknown. This over-saturation may have ramifications for the industry as whole.

Consumer end storage

The increased use of cloud computing could lead to a reduction in demand for high storage capacity consumer end devices, due to cheaper low storage devices that stream all content via the cloud becoming more popular. In a Wired article, Jake Gardner explains that while unregulated usage is beneficial for IT and tech moguls like Amazon, the anonymous nature of the cost of consumption of cloud usage makes it difficult for business to evaluate and incorporate it into their business plans.

Ambiguity of terminology

Outside of the information technology and software industry, the term "cloud" can be found to reference a wide range of services, some of which fall under the category of cloud computing, while others do not. The cloud is often used to refer to a product or service that is discovered, accessed and paid for over the Internet, but is not necessarily a computing resource. Examples of service that are sometimes referred to as "the cloud" include, but are not limited to, crowd sourcing, cloud printing, crowd funding, cloud manufacturing.

Performance interference and noisy neighbors

Due to its multi-tenant nature and resource sharing, Cloud computing must also deal with the "noisy neighbor" effect. This effect in essence indicates that in a shared infrastructure, the activity of a virtual machine on a neighboring core on the same physical host may lead to increased performance degradation of the VMs in the same physical host, due to issues such as e.g. cache contamination. Due to the fact that the neighboring VMs may be activated or deactivated at arbitrary times, the result is an increased variation in the actual performance of Cloud resources. This effect seems to be dependent also on the nature of the applications that run inside the VMs but also other factors such as scheduling parameters and the careful selection may lead to optimized assignment in order to minimize the phenomenon. This has also led to difficulties in comparing various cloud providers on cost and performance using traditional benchmarks for service and application performance, as the time period and location in which the benchmark is performed can result in widely varied results.[168]This observation has led in turn to research efforts to make cloud computing applications intrinsically aware of changes in the infrastructure so that the application can automatically adapt to avoid failure.

Monopolies and privatization of cyberspace

Philosopher points out that, although cloud computing enhances content accessibility; this access is "increasingly grounded in the virtually monopolistic privatization of the cloud which provides this access". According to him, this access, necessarily mediated through a handful of companies, ensures a progressive privatization of global cyberspace. criticizes the argument purported by supporters of cloud computing that this phenomenon is part of the "natural evolution" of the Internet, sustaining that the quasi-monopolies "set prices at will but also filter the software they provide to give its "universality" a particular twist depending on commercial and ideological interests."

The Future

According to Gartner's Hype cycle, Cloud computing has reached a maturity that leads it into a productive phase. This means that most of the main issues with Cloud computing have been addressed to a degree that Clouds have become interesting for full commercial exploitation. This however does not mean that all the problems listed above have actually been solved, only that the according risks can be tolerated to a certain degree. Cloud computing is therefore still as much a research topic, as it is a market offering.

In 2012 the European Commission has issued an analysis of the relevance of the open research issues for commercial stabilization in which various experts from industry and academia identify in particular the following major concerns:

1. open interoperation across (proprietary) cloud solutions at IaaS, PaaS and SaaS levels
2. managing multi-tenancy at large scale and in heterogeneous environments

3. dynamic and seamless elasticity from in house clouds to public clouds for unusual (scale, complexity) and/or infrequent requirements
4. data management in a cloud environment, taking the technical and legal constraints into consideration

These findings have been refined into a research roadmap proposed by the Cloud Computing Expert Group on Research in December 2012 which tries to lay out a timeline for the identified research topics according to their commercial relevance. With the 8th

Conclusion

Cloud computing is become so fantastic in all levels with all network connecting. These are used for communications but had no internal processing capacities. IT is mostly used in software at a remote location. It is widely in most of the telecommunications companies. As computers become more prevalent, scientists and technologists explored ways to make large scale computing power available to more users through time-sharing experimenting with algorithms to provide the optional use of infra structure, platform and applications to the users. So innovative technologies can be used in this cloud computing.

27

Learning Without Limit

Introduction

Learning means modification of behavior. Change in response of behavior is caused partly or wholly by experience. Munn (1954) has rightly defined learning as "the Process of being modified, more or less permanently, by what happens in the world around us, by what we do, or by what we observe."

Learning depends on

1. Experience of the Learner.
2. Capacity and motivation of the Learning
3. Methods in which the Learning materials are presented to the learner.
4. Meaningful of difficulty of learning task.

Characteristics of Learning (Sunitee Dutt 1960)

5. Learning is purposive of goal oriented
6. Learning is an active process.

7. Learning is an individual.
8. Learning is socially conditioned
9. Learning is transferable.

New Teaching and Learning Tools

Learn more about desire. Learns award winning suite of Learning technology/software designed to enhance the online learning environment. The focus will be on learning environment. Learning objects Repository and more. Discover how this easy to use technology is helping faculty engage students into deeper levels of learning and improving the process of online delivery. Instructions appreciate the familiar, easy-to-use interphone of power point to present collections of digital images; there are alternative solutions that provide several advantages over Microsoft's presentation software web galleries and quick time slideshows can create a more interactive learning experience for students. Video furnace provides an easy to use digital video solution to enhance the delivery of digital content to class rooms. Video furnace provides the tools to create and deliver DVD quality content to the students. The new technology of web promise to rapidly increase our ability to teach in the disciplines with technology student learning rarely result from a singular approach. Universal Design for Learning (UDL) helps to educators respond to student learning changes.

UDL Applications are Digital media, off the shelf and web accessible applications and blending UDL alternatives with more traditional instructions Interactive learning through games and simulations as created by the students for class room and internet learning. A tool on the web like blogs incorporated into a course curriculum to teach research skills.

There are many tools available for evaluating your web pages for accessibility. Learning to use tools and techniques to make working in Photoshop easier and more efficient. Microsoft Power Point effecting significant impact on student achievement, critical thinking and problem solving.

Learning without Limit study by exploring the wider opportunities for enhancing the learning capacity of every child that become possible when a whole staff group works together to create an environment free from limiting effects of ability labels and practices. What happens when staff members officially prescribed practices of predicting or prejudging what any individual children might achieve? when they work, instead, to identify and limits on learning? when they replace the fatilison of ability labels with a more hopeful, powerful and empowering view of learners and learning?

The school grew into a thriving community, with distinctive views of learning, curriculum and pedagogy, monitoring and accountability that found expression in every aspect of school life. The distinctive approach to school development, drawing on learning without limits values and principles. Teachers to capture their experience of learning to work within a learning without limits ethos and provided methodological support to teachers who undertook individual enquiries focused on specific significant aspects of their practice.

Teachers were helped to shape and evaluate their classroom practice in accordance with their growing understanding of how they can strengthen and transform children's learning capacity. The school became a professional learning community working within the framework of government requirements and committed to fostering learning capacities. The Children were helped across the school to become active agents in the development of their own and each other's learning capacities. Parents and the wider community became involved in and committed to the process of fostering the learning capacity of all young people.

Support for professional learning

A core leadership task at Wrotham was to create the conditions for professional learning to flourish across the whole school. This was an absolute priority the process of building a school environment inspired by learning without limits. Core ideas and principles was dependent upon the ongoing learning of the whole staff team. It was a process of continuous development and constant renewal, as staff deepened and enriched their understanding of what liberates or limits children's capacity of learn, and reshaped their practices accordingly.

Kind of professional Learning

As clear Patterns emerged in the choices of structures and strategies introduced to support and foster this process it became apparent that they promoted a particular kind of professional learning, recognizing colleagues as active thinkers in their own right, who can and must do their own thinking if worthwhile learning is to take place. Strategies were chosen for their capacity to nurture key dispositions, for example openness, questioning and inventiveness, that feed and sustain autonomous professional judgment and enable people to do the kinds of thinking upon which teaching for learning without limits depends.

The power of passion

The ultimate test of these strategies was whether they helped to strengthen people's sense of passionate Endeavour, to increase their sense of their own agency, their ability to imagine and bring about worthwhile changes through their own efforts. The school-wide culture of learning helped to suture and sustain their passion, cultivating shared energy, passion and hope were harnessed to a shared sense of what they were striving to create together: a school environment in which everybody's learning could flourish, free from the damaging effects of ability labels and ability-focused practice.

Conclusion

Learning to learn is essential and learning is more important than teaching. Learning is also a continuous process. It is life long, it is apt to be equivalent with education. Through education students learn how to learn, learn how to keep on learning, learn how to be creative and innovative, and learn how to contribute meaningfully and significantly to solving the new problems that are encountered in day to day world. The teacher identifies the pupils needs and provide facilities for promoting his cognitive, co native and affective development.

28

Awareness of Flip Teaching Among School Teachers

Introduction

The Flip classroom is the latest learning model to have taken the teaching and training world by storm. The investigator adopted the survey method and target population was the school teachers who are teaching in various boards such as Matriculation and CBSE in and around Madurai district. The size of the sample of the present study is 60 school teachers. The self made check list was used in the study and it consists of 20 items. Statistical technique used are Calculating mean value,'t' test. The Findings are there is no Awareness of flip teaching among school teachers in and around Madurai District and there is no significant difference in the awareness of flip teaching among school teachers with regard to the gender and Board of Institution.

"A Quality education has the power to transform societies in a single generation, provide children with the protection they need from the hazards of poverty, labor exploitation and disease and give them the knowledge, skills and confidence to reach their full potential". India needs multi-dimensional and broad based quality education to maintain its leader ship in the 21st century. Therefore India should show the concern over the quality in education as the education in India is not competitive in terms of the quality with other countries. The FLIP classroom is the latest learning model to have taken the teaching and training world by storm.

In a flipped classroom content normally delivered in lectures is covered by students in their own time, often through the use of video or readings. Face-to-face time is used for activities where the focus is on learning through experience. It allows teachers and trainers to flip through concepts, which in turn gives them more time to interact with students instead of lecturing. This is also known as backwards classroom, reverse instruction, flipping the classroom and reverse teaching. The flip classroom is ideal for adult education and training, where students are more self-motivated and focused. This model of learning compliments training objectives which are 'actionable' rather than passive objectives like 'awareness or comprehension'.

Significance of the Study

This study is undertaken to find out the awareness of flip teaching among school teachers in and around Madurai District. This study gave them the clear knowledge about Flip teaching is a form of blended learning in which students learn new content online by watching video lectures, usually at home, and what used to be homework (assigned problems) is now done in class with teachers offering more personalized guidance and interaction with students, instead of lecturing. This is also known as backwards classroom, flipped classroom, reverse teaching, and the Thayer Method

Background of the Study

This study was done in and around Madurai city. The need of today is quality of education. If the quality is maintained in all the above we can produce professionally skillful students who are going to the meet the future global citizens. So it is necessary to have innovative teaching methods or alternative methods in imparting knowledge among the students. The traditional pattern of teaching has been to assign students to read textbooks and work on problem sets outside school, while listening to lectures and taking tests in class.

Traditionally, the teacher engages with the students who ask questions — but those who don't ask tend to need the most attention. "We refer to 'silent failers,'" said one teacher, claiming that flipping allows her to target those who need the most help rather than the most confident. Flipping changes teachers from "sage on the stage" to "guide on the side", allowing them to work with individuals or groups of students throughout the session. The Investigator wanted to know whether there is awareness of flip teaching among school teachers in and around Madurai District

Objectives of the study

1. To measure and find out whether there is awareness of flip teaching among school teachers in and around Madurai District
2. To enable the teachers to sensitize the today's need to turn towards the flip teaching and classrooms.

Hypotheses

1. Awareness of flip teaching among school teachers in and around Madurai District are high
2. There is significant difference in the awareness of flip teaching among school teachers with regard to the board of institution. [Matriculation and CBSE]
3. There is significant difference in the awareness of flip teaching among school teachers with regard to the gender. [Male & Female]

Methodology used

The survey method was taken and target population is the school teachers who are teaching in various boards such as Matriculation and CBSE in and around Madurai district. The size of the samples of the present study is 60 teachers.

Tool Construction

The self made check list was used to find out whether there is awareness of flip teaching among school teachers in and around Madurai District. The checklist had 20 items

Administration of the Tool

The photocopies of the check-list were distributed to the teachers of four educational institutions in and around Madurai. The filled in questionnaires were corrected analyzed and interpreted.

Statistical Technique Used

Calculating mean value,'t' test

Table shows the number of teachers from four schools

S.no	Name of the school	Institution	Total no	F	M
(1)	S.S.V.Sala	Matriculation	15	15	-
(2)	Le Chatlier	Matriculation	15		15
(3)	PVK Academy	CBSE	15	8	7
(4)	Vellammal	CBSE	15	7	8
		Total	60	30	30

Hypothesis: 1

4. Awareness of flip teaching among school teachers in and around Madurai District are high

Table Showing the Mean Value

Name of the school	Total no	Sex		Board	Over All Mean
		Female	Male		
S.S.V.Sala	15	15	-	Matriculation	7.5
Le Chatlier	15		15	Matriculation	9
PVK Academy	15	8	7	CBSE	8.5
Vellammal	15	7	8	CBSE	9.5

It is inferred from the above table that there is no Awareness of flip teaching among school teachers in and around Madurai District. All the mean scores indicated that they are less than the theoretical mean (10). Still there were no innovative teaching methods were followed to reach the global standard as well as to improve the low achievers.

Hypothesis: 2

5. There is significant difference in the awareness of flip teaching among school teachers with regard to the board of institution. [Matriculation and CBSE]

Table showing the difference between the variables

S.No	Variable	Mean	Std.dev	't'	Significance at 0.5 level
1	Matriculation	8.25	0.50	0.93	No Significant
2	CBSE	9	0.74		

6. It is inferred from the above table that the't' value is 0.93 is lesser than the't' value 1.96 at 0.5 level of significance. So the research hypothesis is rejected. The result indicated that there is no significant difference in the awareness of flip teaching among school teachers with regard to the board of institution. [Matriculation and CBSE]

Hypothesis: 3

7. There is significant difference in the awareness of flip teaching among school teachers with regard to the gender. [Male & Female]

Table showing the difference between the variables

S.NO	Variable	mean	Std.dev	't'	Significance at 0.5 level
1	Female	8.5	1.25	0.98	No Significant
2	male	9	0.57		

It is inferred from the above table that the't' value is 0.98 is lesser than the't' value 1.96 at 0.5 level of significance. So the research hypothesis is rejected. The result indicated that there is no significant difference in the awareness of flip teaching among school teachers with regard to the gender. [Male & Female]

Hypotheses Verification

8. There is significant difference in the awareness of flip teaching among school teachers with regard to the board of institution. [Matriculation and CBSE] is rejected.

9. There is significant difference in the awareness of flip teaching among school teachers with regard to the gender. [Male & Female] is rejected.

Delimitation

The samples are taken from only from four schools in and around Madurai area and also restricted to the variable that is type of institution and gender alone. In this study the Investigator use only mean and‘t’ test as the statistical treatment .This was also delimitation.

Scope of the Study

This study can highlight the need for the alternative, creative, student friendly, user friendly and innovative methods of teaching. The flip classroom is the latest learning model to have taken the teaching and training world by storm. The flip teaching models are being incorporated by teachers of all subjects, for students of all ages. This mode of learning is now slowly making inroads into the teaching and training in India. The flip classroom is ideal for adult education and training, where students are more self-motivated and focused. This model of learning compliments training objectives which are ‘actionable’ rather than passive objectives like ‘awareness or comprehension’.

Suggestion for the Future

1. We can take more schools for the study
2. We can take so many variables
3. We can also use extend all the boards of schools in future.

Educational Implications

This Study revealed that there is a need for considering another scenario where in students has already gone through a video lecture on the second conditional at their own time. They can rewind, pause and repeat the lecture as many times as they want. Additionally, they do graded exercises to practice the concept and take up an assessment to check their proficiency. Both the learner and the facilitator now know what to focus on and the class is much more productive for the learner. The facilitator only has to provide solutions for problem areas. Flip training can help overcome the constraints and make learning a focused and productive experience for the learner

29

The Flipped Classroom: the Latest Technology for Teachers

Introduction

The Latest Technology for Teachers. All across the nation and beyond, teachers are experimenting with flipping the classroom. They are flipping instruction. The basic concept is quite simple. Homework gets done in the class work while class instruction occurs at home. With the flipped classroom concept, the teacher becomes less of a "sage on the stage" and more of a "guide on the side." This is done by having students watch pre-recorded lessons on screen or pod casts online at home. The next day, class lecture time is freed up to have the students put their newly acquired knowledge into practice.

Technology has changed the way of doing everything, and education is no exception. Flipping the classroom can be as simple or as elaborate as the teacher wants to make it. Low-tech teachers can flip classroom instruction with a simple-made video he or she makes, or choose one from shared files. High-tech teachers will explore software and technologies to enhance the flipped classroom learning experience. This enhancement can be in the way of shareware such as Edmodo or learnspace. These sites are like having face book accounts private to you and your students. Teachers can post quizzes, due dates, etc. on line. Students can post and form groups for working on projects together. Files too large to share by email can be sent.

Videos can be viewed on computers, laptops, iPads Smartphones, etc. Students with no computer access (rare these days) can be given a spot in the classroom, computer lab or media center. This is also a good place for students who may need to review the material while in school.

The Flipped Class: What it is and what it is not

There has been a lot of interest in the flipped classroom.

The traditional definition of a flipped class is: Where videos take the place of direct instruction

- This then allows students to get individual time in class to work with their teacher on key learning activities.
- It is called the flipped class because what used to be class work (the "lecture" is done at home via teacher-created videos and what used to be homework (assigned problems) is now done in class.

But from our perspective, as successful flipped teachers, everyone believe it is so much more. People also realize there is a lot of mis-information about the Flipped Classroom and quite a bit of controversy about whether or not this is a viable instructional methodology. Thus the purpose of this article is to list out what one believes it is and what one believes it is not.

The Flipped Classroom is NOT

A synonym for online videos. When most people hear about the flipped class all they think about are the videos. It is the interaction and the meaningful learning activities that occur during the face-to-face time that is most important.

1. About replacing teachers with videos.

2. An online course.
3. Students working without structure.
4. Students spending the entire class staring at a computer screen.
5. Students working in isolation.

The Flipped Classroom IS

A means to INCREASE interaction and personalized contact time between students and teachers.

1. An environment where students take responsibility for their own learning.
2. A classroom where the teacher is not the "sage on the stage", but the "guide on the side".
3. A blending of direct instruction with constructivist learning.
4. A classroom where students who are absent due to illness or extra-curricular activities such as athletics or field-trips, don't get left behind.
5. A class where content is permanently archived for review or remediation.
6. A class where all students are engaged in their learning.
7. A place where all students can get a personalized education.

The flipped classroom seems to be the latest buzz in educational trends. Is this truly a new revolutionary approach or a revision of a technique used throughout the ages? To be clear, in simplest terms, flipping the classroom refers to swapping classroom lecture time for hands-on practice time. So the lecture is done for homework usually via a video or audio file and the classroom time is spent clarifying and applying new knowledge gained.

A survey of the latest literature indicates that flipping a classroom is not a new idea. It is the way that idea is applied that is gaining so much attention and in most cases, so much praise. Many say that reversing the content delivery and practice is a decades old practice. Consider literature classes where the student reads the novel outside of class. Class time is spent discussing themes and archetypes and rarely the plot of the story. Law schools also traditionally flip when students participate in Socratic seminars and must prepare ahead of time to effectively participate in the seminar and have knowledge to back up their statements (Berrett, 2012). So if it is not something new in education, why is it attracting headlines and discussions?

First a little history on the recent re-emergence of this time tested class technique. It seems that the confluence of enlightenment that led to the current use of the term "flipped classroom" originates in three or four different situations. While high school science teachers Jonathan Bergmann and Aaron Sams of Woodland Park, CO are most often credited with coining the phrase flipped classroom in 2007 (White, 2011), there are other schools and programs that essentially developed the same concept around the same time, albeit after.

Dr. Eric Mazur, a physicist at Harvard University, has been using the method for 21 years. With the addition of assistive technology to allow for student response and feedback during the peer instruction session, attendees saw how this process works to maximize time with the instructor and focus on higher order thinking skills rather than just taking notes and regurgitating facts.

Some of the characteristics of this latest iteration include engaging the students on a higher level and a smaller ratio of students to instructors while working within the economics of education. As Dr. Mazur said: "Once you engaged the students' minds, there's an eagerness to learn, to be right, to master" (Berrett, 2012). According to Bloom (1984), "an average student who receives one-on-one attention is enabled by constant feedback and corrective process, and can jump into the 98th percentile of the student population in academic achievement" (Houston and Lin, 2012). This was stated 24 years ago but most classes are still taught with teacher-centered lectures and only the persistent students seek out one-on-one assistance.

Lecture as a teaching technique is not going away. Economics dictate that class size will not decrease to lower the student-to-instructor ratio. Therefore, lecturing makes economic sense. Flipping and moving the lecture to the homework realm and saving application and one-on-one work for the classroom experience makes the lecture model more productive. Implementing a flipped classroom enables more focused teaching and learning to take place in the classroom.

Effectively flipping a classroom brings many benefits. Flipping uses technology to remove passive, one-way lecturing as the only means of teaching. Thus, the instructor and students can interact within the newly gained instructional time (Houston and Lin, 2012). The increase of teacher-student interaction during class time is what characterizes its success (White, 2012). The classroom time is used to solve problems and apply to other contexts (the application of higher order thinking skills).

Flipping the classroom also makes differentiating instruction based on students' needs easier because everyone does not necessarily need to do the same task in class (Liles, 2012). Simply looking at the perceived and real benefits of flipping as well as the amount of research recently done should be incentive to consider a flip as a great way to reach students and approach mastery of content.

Transformational Potential of Flipped Classrooms

In The Flipped Classroom, the Teacher Is Available to Guide Students as they apply what they have learned online. One of the drawbacks of traditional homework is that students don't receive meaningful feedback on their work while they are doing it; they may have no opportunity to relearn concepts they struggled to master. With a teacher present to answer questions and watch over how students are doing, the feedback cycle has greater potential to bolster student learning.

The flipped classroom does not address all the limitations of the brick-and-mortar school. Although in the best flipped-classroom implementations, each student can move at her own pace and view lessons at home that meet her individual needs rather than those of the entire class, most flipped classrooms do not operate this way. As Salman Khan, the media's personification of the flipped-classroom, observes in The One World Schoolhouse, "Although it makes class time more interactive and lectures more independent, the 'flipped classroom' still has students moving together in age-based cohorts at roughly the same pace, with snapshot exams that are used more to label students than address their weaknesses" (see "To YouTube and Beyond," book reviews, Summer 2013).

This arrangement also doesn't tackle the root causes of the lack of motivation that persists among many low-achieving students.

Some in the media have suggested that the flipped-classroom approach may only work in upper-income, suburban schools. If low-income students lack access to computers at home or to reliable Internet access, flipping may be a nonstarter in some schools. If students can't benefit from online instruction at home, then they need to receive instruction in the classroom or risk falling behind. Some fear that in relying on parents to provide technology and support, the flipped-classroom model may exacerbate existing resource inequalities. Schools can make computer labs available during after school hours, however, and parental assistance is less critical when watching an online video than when solving homework problems.

What is perhaps most telling is that the "no-excuses" charter schools that serve large numbers of low-income students well—KIPP, Rocket ship, Alliance, and Summit among them—are not flipping their classrooms. Even as these schools adopt blended-learning models, the flipped classroom isn't among them. The models these schools are employing give students more support as they need it and actively guide students to more ownership over their learning. These models also do not rely on students having access to high-speed Internet-connected computers at home; online learning occurs during the school day.

Even if the flipped classroom does prove of some benefit to some low-income students, this change in structure alone is unlikely to produce the vast improvement in student learning our country needs.

But that doesn't mean the innovation is insignificant. The flipped classroom might still have an important indirect impact on the American education system, as one brand of digital learning. The optimal use of digital learning will vary in different contexts and communities. Some people will attend full-time virtual schools, with even the “classroom” experience occurring online; most will attend brick-and-mortar schools that employ some version of digital learning.

Unlike school vouchers for low-income students, charter schools in disadvantaged communities, or bonus pay for teachers in inner-city schools, digital learning is not designed for just one slice of the population. It’s not a policy that parents might support in theory but, because it has no practical impact on them, won’t spend political energy promoting or defending. Rather, if it works as well as its proponents hope, digital learning will gather political support from a wide swath of the American public. And it may well turn out that the flipped classroom is most effective in private schools or upper-income suburban schools. If that’s how those students make the best use of digital learning, that’s OK. As Khan says, “Blue jeans didn’t become cool until Hollywood started wearing them.” In the world of digital learning, the flipped classroom may just be one good brand.

The purpose of flipping the classroom is to shift from passive to active learning to focus on the higher order thinking skills such as analysis, synthesis and evaluation (Bloom). As explained in this short video, Flipping the Classroom: Simply Speaking (Penn State), students access key content individually (or in small groups) prior to class time and then meet face-to-face in the larger group to explore content through active learning and engagement strategies.

There are many permutations of what a flipped classroom will look like and depends on variables such as class size, resources, support and readiness to change. At UQ, several teachers across the faculties have already flipped their classrooms and their valuable experiences have been captured in the Studies section.

In the flipped classroom, the roles and expectations of students and teachers change where: students take more responsibility for their own learning and study core content either individually or in groups before class and then apply knowledge and skills to a range of activities using higher order thinking, teaching ‘one-to-many’ focuses more on facilitation and moderation than lecturing, though lecturing is still important. Significant learning opportunities can be gained through facilitating active learning, engaging students, guiding learning, correcting misunderstandings and providing timely feedback using a variety of pedagogical strategies, there is a greater focus on concept exploration, meaning making and demonstration or application of knowledge in the face-to-face setting (see Diagram 1 below).

Diagram 1: Learning opportunities of the flipped classroom (adapted from Gerstein) Educational technologies (see Diagram 2) are an important feature of the flipped classroom as they can be used to:

- **capture key content** for students to access at their own convenience and to suit their pace of learning (e.g. lecture material, readings, interactive multimedia),
- **present learning materials** in a variety of formats to suit different learner styles (e.g. text, videos, audio, multimedia),
- **provide opportunities for discourse** and interaction in and out of class (e.g. polling tools, discussion tools, content creation tools),
- **convey timely information**, updates and reminders for students (e.g micro-blogging, announcement tools),
- **provide immediate and anonymous feedback** for teachers and students (e.g. quizzes, polls) to signal revision points,
- **capture data** about students to analyse their progress and identify 'at risk' students (e.g. analytics).

Diagram 2: Key elements of a flipped classroom (Strayer)

Sample Plan for Flipped Instruction

The objective is to understand and apply the scientific method. Students will identify dependent variable, independent variable, control group, hypothesis,

1. Build motivation and create a "hook" for anticipating learning with a PowerPoint presentation or text book reading. Include a short quiz either online or with pencil/paper. Whatever your

level of technology is at this point. Don't worry, there is no need to be a techie to do this. Give points for completing the presentation.

2. Create or import a lesson/lecture on the basics of the scientific method. It's a good beginning. It is best if you make these videos yourself, but it's OK to use other videos Check for understanding with a quiz, online or paper/pencil.
3. Review with questioning at the beginning or class
4. Assign directions for a project:
5. Purpose: Create a lab to demonstrate the scientific method using a simple paper airplane.
6. Make a hypothesis: Decide on a plan and make a prediction based on the procedure you have developed to use the paper airplane.
7. Develop a plan that demonstrates the scientific method. Try to create a table and a graph to record collected data. Have students do 10 trials.
8. Have students write two paragraphs analyzing collected data.

Advantages of Flipped Instruction

Flipped instruction can be used in almost any classroom to a degree. Just remember the basic concept. Classroom instruction becomes homework and homework becomes classroom work. This frees up much time for active learning in the classroom. Teachers can plan hands-on activities for students that will allow them to develop higher-order thinking skills. Some of the ways to actively engage students in the classroom after viewing lectures on video are as follows.

1. class discussions
2. debates
3. think-pair-share
4. cooperative learning

5. surveys and polls
6. graphing and displaying data
7. visual arts projects
8. low or high tech presentations
9. experiments
10. research projects

Unlike classroom lectures, online lessons can be reviewed from as far back as the beginning of the lesson if necessary. They can even be reviewed before major exams. Parents will love having the change in homework. Struggling through trying to work problems or answer questions about forgotten classroom lectures is eliminated. They can even view the videos themselves in order to be better able to help children understand the lesson content.

Although the flipped classroom is relatively new, results of studies are showing improvements across the board from better test scores to lowered drop-out rates in schools that have implemented flipped instruction.

Final Thoughts on the Flipped Classroom

Have fun with this cool new idea. Start off slowly if you are "tech shy." Just remember the basic idea of the flipped classroom, and it will make sense. It could turn your teaching right side up and make more sense to you and your students.

Flipping the classroom has transformed our teaching practice. We no longer stand in front of our students and talk at them for thirty to sixty minutes at a time. This radical change has allowed us to take on a different role with our students. Both of us taught for many years (a combined thirty-seven years) using this model. We were both good teachers. In fact, Jonathan received the Presidential Award for Excellence in Math and Science Teaching while being the sage on the stage, and Aaron received the same award under the Flipped model. Though as we look back, we could never go back to teaching in the traditional manner.

The flipped classroom has not only changed our classrooms, but many teachers from around the world have adopted the model and are using it to teach Spanish, Science, Math, elementary, middle, high school, and adults. We have presented all over North America and have seen how flipping your classroom can change kids' lives.

Flipping Increases Student Interaction

One of the greatest benefits of flipping is that overall interaction increases: Teacher to student and student to student. Since the role of the teacher has changed from presenter of content to learning coach, we spend our time talking to kids. We are answering questions, working with small groups, and guiding the learning of each student individually.

When students are working on an assignment and we notice a group of students who are struggling with the same thing, we automatically organize the students into a tutorial group. We often conduct mini-lectures with groups of students who are struggling with the same content. The beauty of these mini-lectures is we are delivering "just in time" instruction when the students are ready for learning.

Since the role of the teacher has changed, to more of a tutor than a deliverer of content, we have the privilege of observing students interact with each other. As we roam around the class, we notice the students developing their own collaborative groups. Students are helping each other learn instead of relying on the teacher as the sole disseminator of knowledge. It truly is magical to observe. We are often in awe of how well our students work together and learn from each other.

Some might ask how we developed a culture of learning. We think the key is for students to identify learning as their goal, instead of striving for the completion of assignments. We have purposely tried to make our classes places where students carry out meaningful activities instead of completing busy work. When we respect our students in this way, they usually respond. They begin to realize, and for some it takes time, that we are here to guide them in their learning instead of being the authoritative pedagogue. Our goal is for them to be the best learner possible, and to truly understand the content in our classes. When our students grasp the concept that we are on their side, they respond by doing their best.

Flipping Changes the Way We Talk with Parents

We both remember sitting in parent conferences for years and parents would often ask us how their son or daughter behaved in class. What they were really asking was does my son or daughter sit quietly, act respectfully, raise their hand, and not disturb other students. These traits are certainly good for all to learn, but we struggled answering this question when we first started flipping the classroom.

You see, the question is a non-issue in our classroom. Since students are coming with the primary focus on learning, the real question is now: Is your student learning or not? If they are not learning, what can we do to help them learn? This is a much more profound question and when we can discuss this with parents, we can really move students into a place which will help them become better learners.

There are a myriad of reasons why a student is not learning well. Do students have some missing background knowledge? Do students have personal issues that interfere with their learning? Or are students more concerned with "playing school" rather than learning. When the parents and teachers can diagnose why the child is not learning we create a powerful moment where the necessary interventions can be implemented.

1. References

Alvarez, B. (2011). Flipping the classroom: homework in class, lessons at home. Learning First, Retrieved from http://www.learningfirst.org/flipping-classroom-homework-class-lessons-home

2. Bergmann, J.; Sams, A. (2008) Remixing chemistry class. *Learning and Leading with Technology.* 36(4) 24-27.
3. Berrett, D. (2012). How 'flipping' the classroom can improve the traditional lecture. *The Chronicle of Higher Education,* Retrieved from http://chronicle.com/article/How-Flipping-the-Classroom/130857/

4. Houston, M., & Lin, L. (2012, March). Humanizing the classroom by flipping the homework versus lecture equation. Paper presented at Society for information technology & teacher education international conference (site) 2012, Austin, TX.

5. Liles, M. (2012, April 10). [Web log message]. Retrieved from http://blog.discoveryeducation.com/blog/2012/04/10/flip-your-classroom-with-iscovery-education/

6. November, A. (2012). Flipped learning: a response to fie common criticisms. November Learning, Retrieved from http://novemberlearning.com/resources/archive-of-articles/flipped-learning-a-response-to-five-common-criticisms/

7. White, D. (2011). Literature justification for blended/reverse instruction. Unpublished raw data, Liberty University, Lynchburg, Virginia.-See more at: http://www. faculty focus.com/articles/teaching-with-technology-articles/understanding-the-flipped-classroom-part-1/#sthash. l9AP3NVx.dpuf

30

A Study of Online Teaching among School Students

Introduction

Blended Learning is a formal education program in which a student learns at least in part through online delivery of content and instruction with some element of student control over time, place, path, or pace. In the growing technology, this scenario plays a major role in teaching and learning. The Learners, Learning methods, learning approaches, Learning situations and the teachers all have to be accessed with the online learning or Teaching.

As all the Learners of all the fields are depending on the Information Technology in our day today life, one needs to have the knowledge about the blended learning for self development among all major fields of learning. Education plays a major role with this blended learning, as the class room is the place which determines the future of every child and the Nation. In this Y-Generation, everything is easily learnt though online. For example; Driving, Cooking, Marketing, Shopping and ticketing...etc

Review

The Concept of blended learning has been around for a longtime, but the terminology was not firmly established until 21st century. In 1999, the Interactive learning centers, announced its change of name to EPIC learning.

In 2006, the first handbook of Blended Learning by Book and Graham was published. Graham defined "blended as the learning system, combining of internet, digital media with established classroom forms that require the physical co presence of teacher and students.

In 2007, Clark & Westcott stated that Podcasting consists of listening to audio recordings of lectures. It can be used to review live lectures and to provide opportunities for students to rehearse oral presentations.

In 2009, Mc Garr and in 2009 again Steven & Teasley studied that Podcasts may also provide supplemental information to enhance traditional lectures.

In 2009, Callaway & Ewen said the Psychological researches suggest that university students who download podcast lectures achieve substantially higher exam results than those who attend the lectures in person.

Word Usage and Context

In current research literature, the word blended learning are often used interchangeably as, blended, Hybrid, Technology- Mediated Instruction, web-enhanced Instruction and Mixed-Mode Instruction...Etc however the united states use the term often blended learning and mixed mode instruction with more regularity in recent researches.

Objectives

1. To study simultaneous independent and collaborative learning experiences.
2. To study the incorporation of major contributions in lecture or teaching.

3. To study the incorporation of information technology into the class project.
4. To study the incorporation of communication between teachers and students.
5. To study the evaluation of students understanding of course material
6. To study the development of interest and creativity of students in online teaching.

Hypotheses

1. There is a simultaneous independent and collaborate learning experience would be in favorable mode for present days educational streamline
2. There is a significant relationship in blended learning on interest and success (achievement).
3. There is a relationship between lectures and students.
4. There is significant relationship in student understanding in online evaluation.
5. There is a significant relationship among interest and creativity of using information technology.

Methodology

The following questionnaire is prepared in order to study the use of online teaching and

learning among B.Ed Students.

1. How far the mobile / internet browsing help in you development?

   Yes/Fair/No

2. How far the information technologies help in doing your project and homework?

   Yes/Fair/No

3. Is getting education related information is easy to access from mobile internet?

Yes/Fair/No

4. Is getting educational related information is easy to access from computer internet?

Yes/Fair/No

5. How far the knowledge of computer helps you in initiating your creativity and interest?

Yes/Fair/No

6. How far the e-communication helps to learn?

Yes/Fair/No

Blended Learning Result Analysis

	Good	Fair	No
Total	555	190	55
Percentage(%)	69.375	23.75	6.875

Recommendations:

1. For lower achievers and average students the online teaching method would be more useful as they can save the information and learn whenever they can but it is not possible with the teacher.
2. Online teaching helps to develop the interest of all children through animation and graphics which the teacher or the Blackboard cannot provide.
3. Self learning for lower achievers is more possible in online learning.
4. Based on the level of learning, one can be promoted to the higher level of learning with their interest and area of knowledge.
5. Time and place of learning or any other factors are not a limit for learning through online.

6. One can save time and duration through online learning.
7. Easy to access all information through online from any corner of the world.

Conclusion

Thus the Blended learning combines brick and mortar schooling with online delivery of content and instruction. Mobile devices provide support that enhances teaching and learning in a virtual class room environment and educational experiences. Blended learning takes the classroom out of a traditional brick and mortar setting. The students become the part of virtual communities used for collaboration. Blended learning transitions away from a traditional teaching environment to a customized and interactive web platform for the user. The proponents of blended learning cite the opportunities for data collections and customization of instruction and assessment as two major benefits of this approach. Schools with blended learning models may also choose to reallocate resources to boost student achievement outcomes.